1 Corinthians
Personal Workbook

By Chad Sychtysz

Published by
Spiritbuilding Publishers
9700 Ferry Road, Waynesville, Ohio 45068

1 CORINTHIANS PERSONAL WORKBOOK
By Chad Sychtysz

ISBN: 978–1955285–94–0

Spiritbuilding
PUBLISHERS

spiritbuilding.com

Table of Contents

The author of this workbook can be contacted at chad@booksbychad.com.

Cover design by Larissa Lynch

Introduction to *1 Corinthians*

Unquestionably, the apostle Paul's epistle to the Corinthians (*1 Corinthians*) is one of the most important and influential books of the New Testament (NT). This epistle is a rich example of Paul's loving patience toward—and forthright admonition of—a mixed group of people who have only recently converted to Christ. Some of these people are Jews, far more are Greeks (Gentiles), but all of them are still learning to live like *Christians*. Paul needed an expert balance of both encouragement and correction, and this letter is proof that he had struck such a balance. Because of this fine contribution to the NT, we have excellent guidance on how to maintain this same balance in our own churches.

The City of Corinth: Corinth ["ornament"] was an important commercial city of ancient Greece, being ideally situated on the western end of the isthmus between the Peloponnesian peninsula and the European mainland. It was strategically positioned at the

intersection of north–south land trade routes *and* east–west sea trade routes, providing safe passage between the Aegean and Adriatic Seas.[1]

Corinth's beginnings date as far back as the seventh century BC. During the third and fourth centuries BC, it remained under Macedonian control. In 196 BC, the city received limited autonomy by Rome, but it rebelled against Roman rule only fifty years later. As a result of this, Rome thoroughly destroyed the city (146 BC), and it became a sparsely populated ruin for one hundred years. In 46 BC, Julius Caesar declared Corinth a Roman colony, rebuilt the city, it rapidly regained its prominence as well as unprecedented prosperity.[2] Unfortunately, its paganism, hedonism, and wickedness also flourished; the term "Corinthian" became synonymous with gross immorality in the Mediterranean world. The city was also steeped in idolatry and temple prostitution: Apollo, Poseidon, Athena, and Aphrodite were among some of the principal gods worshiped there.[3]

Author and Date of Writing: There has never been any serious questioning of Paul's authorship of this letter.[4] Its text raises no major concerns; its canonicity (or, placement in the sacred writings deemed inspired by God) has never been an issue with early church scholars and historians.[5] The apostle Paul first visited Corinth on his second missionary journey (Acts 18:1ff) in AD 51 or 52. Corinth's coarse reputation and brash immorality were undoubtedly intimidating to Paul. In fact, it seemed an unlikely place for the gospel to succeed, but Jesus told Paul not to be afraid, "for I am with you, … and I have many people in this city" (Acts 18:10). As a result of this encouragement, Paul established a church in Corinth and remained there for eighteen months (Acts 18:11).

After he left Corinth, Paul began hearing from trustworthy sources that there were divisions within its church. There was a certain element among the Corinthian believers that had arrogantly concluded that they no longer needed Paul's instruction, even though they conducted themselves with spiritual immaturity. About this same time, the Corinthians had written to Paul with questions concerning various issues (including marriage, spiritual gifts, and the resurrection). These two situations—the divisions (and those who caused them) and the written questions—were the occasion for the writing of what we call *1 Corinthians*.

Paul's earnest intention was to revisit Corinth, but he sent Timothy and Erastus to them first (Acts 19:22, 1 Cor. 16:5–11), and Titus. (Many believe Titus delivered this first epistle to the Corinthians.) Paul waited anxiously for word from Titus as to how the Corinthians received this letter (2 Cor. 2:12–13) since it dealt with difficult topics and required him to use strong language at times. After an agonizing delay, Paul finally learned that the Corinthians (in general) had received his letter in the spirit in which he had written it and had repented of their sins (2 Cor. 7:6–9). There remained, however, a group of "false apostles" who challenged Paul's apostolic authority (2 Cor. 11:12–13), and Paul's response to these men occupies much of the epistle we know as *2 Corinthians*. To our knowledge, Paul did not actually visit Corinth again until after the writing of this second epistle.

Paul spent nearly three years in Ephesus (Acts 20:32), and near the end of this period is when it is believed that he wrote *1 Corinthians*. In that letter, he said that he would remain in Ephesus until the coming Pentecost (late spring), and then would make a roundabout trip to Corinth by way of Macedonia (16:5–8). This puts the date of writing no later than the early spring of AD 57, about a year before his arrest in Jerusalem.

Purpose and Theme: In his letter, Paul revealed the Corinthians to be a very worldly–minded people struggling to adapt to a holy, spiritual existence. Re–educating the worldly, sensual–minded Corinthians to think and act like Christians was a difficult process; even after all of Paul's instruction, the Corinthians continued to grapple with their deeply imbedded paganism.[6] These people still had only a limited exposure to the teaching of the gospel, and some had come out of deviant lifestyles (6:9–11).[7] Furthermore, they did not have a copy of the NT to reference as we do today. They did, however, have miraculous gifts by which to receive prophecies, confirmation of divine truth, and other needed information. Yet, even with this, they remained "fleshly" in their thinking (3:2–3). They had problems with leadership (or the lack of it), schisms, social/cultural influences, moral issues, church assembly decorum, and doctrinal teachings. Specifically, they:

❑ were prone to the petty and divisive spirit that is common among the ungodly (1:10–17).
❑ gravitated to the sophisticated oratory style of Greek rhetoricians rather than the simplicity of the gospel of Christ—the "word of the cross" (chapters 1–2).
❑ tended to put more stock in mere *men* than in Christ (chapter 3). In doing so, they threatened to undermine the work of their own congregation.
❑ prided themselves on being independently wise, and therefore no longer in need of Paul's instruction (chapter 4). Yet, their actions betrayed this, as they continued to think in a way that was spiritually immature and short–sighted.
❑ allowed an immoral situation to go unreprimanded in their own midst, despite their claim to wisdom and maturity (chapter 5).
❑ would rather take their own brothers in Christ to a secular court rather than to allow wise Christian men to decide matters of justice for them (6:1–11).

- did not see the grave danger of immorality (6:12–20) but assumed that what was done in the body had little bearing upon their spiritual well-being.
- had several questions about marriage (and celibacy), including the marriage of a believer with an unbeliever (chapter 7).
- prided themselves on their knowledge of God at the expense of the conscience of their fellow brother in the Lord (chapter 8).
- misunderstood the use of Christian liberties (chapter 9).
- thought themselves to be immune to the seduction of pride, the deception of their heart, and the temptation of idolatry (chapter 10).
- misunderstood (and/or had questions on) the role of women in the assembly (11:1–16).
- turned the Lord's Supper into a common meal—an event in which they divided over class, economic status, and other worldly distinctions (11:17–34).
- boasted in their spiritual gifts rather than use them for the encouragement and edification of the church (chapter 12, 14).
- put more emphasis on temporary gifts than on godly love (chapter 13).
- allowed outside influences, as well as their own misunderstandings, to undermine the reality and importance of the resurrection of the dead (chapter 15).
- had questions on "the collection for the saints" (16:1–4).

While Paul's letter does deal with some issues that are no longer immediately relevant to us (such as the use of miraculous gifts), it provides a wealth of critical instruction to all Christians. It is difficult to imagine our understanding of Christ's church without this information. Not only this, but Christians today continue to grapple with many of the same problems facing the Corinthians: divisions, worldliness, spiritual immaturity, improper use of Christian liberties, the failure to exercise godly love properly, issues dealing with proper conduct and reverence, teachings on the resurrection, etc.

It is hard for us to imagine the weight of responsibility placed upon Paul in having to deal with the childlike mentality of the Corinthian church without coming across as angry, patronizing, or condescending. "We perceive the difficulty of the task imposed upon the Apostle, who must guard from so many perils, and guide through so many difficulties, his children in the faith, whom else he had begotten in vain; and we learn to appreciate more fully the magnitude of that laborious responsibility under which he describes himself as almost ready to sink, 'the care of all the churches.'"[8] We can see God's hand in preparing a man like Paul to deal with a church like the one in Corinth.

Lesson One:

Salutation and Introductory Comments (1:1–17)

Paul identifies himself as "an apostle of Jesus Christ by the will of God," immediately re–establishing his role and authority (1:1). This is important and necessary, since some Corinthians thought they were as knowledgeable or capable as he was, and therefore no longer needed his instruction. Paul reminds them that God "called" him to be an apostle rather than him assuming this office on his own authority (Acts 9:15–16, 26:16–18, and Col. 1:25).

Concerning "Sosthenes," nothing else is known about him unless he is the same man mentioned in Acts 18:17. "However, against this identification is the fact that Sosthenes was a rather common name and there is no evidence linking the two."[9] While Sosthenes gives his endorsement to this letter, Paul remains its true author and wields his own apostolic authority throughout it. It is also possible that Paul dictated this epistle to Sosthenes to write it; regardless, Paul authenticates this with his characteristic signature (16:21).

Recognition of the Corinthian Church (1:2–9): The "church of God which is at Corinth" (1:2) identifies a singular, self–governed *earthly* congregation and not the entire *spiritual* body of Christ (Col. 1:18). Christ's church is comprised of spiritual souls; the church at Corinth is comprised of physical people. The two (Christ's church and the church at Corinth) are not interchangeable, are not in the same context, and do not operate in the exact same way. Christ is the "head" of His church by virtue of His identity (as its Redeemer) and His authority (as the Son of God). Whether He serves as the "head" of the church at Corinth is determined by the faithfulness of those who comprise that congregation. Christ's fellowship (1:9) is not automatic or assumed; it can only be present when people agree to the terms of that fellowship. The synonymous phrases Paul uses to describe the congregation is as follows:

- **"the church of God which is at Corinth":** While "church of Christ" is used only once in Scripture to identify a congregation of believers (Rom. 16:16), "church of God" is used numerous times: Acts 20:28, 1 Cor. 10:32, 11:16, 22, 2 Cor. 1:1, etc.
- **"those who have been sanctified in Christ Jesus":** The collection of Christians at Corinth could not be legitimately recognized by Christ's apostle unless they *belonged* to Christ.
- **"saints by calling":** "Saints" literally means "holy ones,"[10] which describes not only the (ideally) virtuous nature of such people (1 Peter 1:13–16, Rev. 19:8) but also their access to the Father through Christ (Eph. 2:17–19).
- **"those who … call upon … Christ":** To "call upon the name of the Lord" means to appeal to Christ for the salvation that He offers (Acts 4:12).

Paul prayed often for the Corinthians (1:4). He reminds them that "in everything you were enriched in Him [Christ]" (1:5)," since "in Christ" is the source of all spiritual blessings (Eph. 1:3). Such blessings ("gifts") come through His word (2 Tim. 3:16–17), the personal example of Christ (John 13:17), and however God chooses to answer prayers (James 1:5).

"[T]he revelation of our Lord Jesus Christ" (1:7) points to a future event and has no reference in the NT epistles other than the Second Coming of Christ (Phil. 3:20, Col. 3:4, 1 Thess. 1:10, 2:19, 1 Peter 1:7, etc.). Paul consistently regarded Christ's second advent as a real and literal event that will signal the end of the physical world (1 Thess. 4:13–17, 2 Peter 3:3–10). Thus, the same God who calls into fellowship those saved by Christ's grace will see their salvation to its end (1:8–9; see Phil. 1:6). "God is faithful" means He is believable, trustworthy, and dependable; He unfailingly delivers on His promises. He is faithful to Himself, His word, His promises, individual believers, and (collectively) His church.

Divisions in the Church (1:10–17): To "agree [or, speak the same thing]" (1:10) does *not* mean that human consensus is to govern the church at Corinth. The source of all Christian agreement must conform to the doctrine that defines fellowship with God *and* each other. This unity must also be consistent with Christ's own oneness or like–mindedness with His Father (John 17:17–23). It is impossible for people to have unity with God apart from His doctrine, which His Son has revealed to us (Gal. 1:11–12). Thus, maintaining the "same mind" and "same judgment [or, opinion; sentiment[11]]" has a specific reference and context.

Fellowship, unity, one–mindedness, and singularity of purpose are the ideals. However, the Corinthians manifested spiritual immaturity through their quarrels and schisms (1:11).[12] We do not know who "Chloe's people" are, but it seems clear that the apostle learned about the divisions among the Corinthians through a third party.[13] Specifically, the Corinthians were dividing themselves by the men who baptized them (1:12). Thus, individual members placed greater emphasis on human distinctions rather than give all glory to Christ (see 1:30–31). "Apollos" is undoubtedly the man of the same name in Acts 18:24–28; being a skilled orator, he would have had a certain appeal to the Greeks in Corinth who put great confidence in the ability to speak eloquently and proficiently. "Cephas" is the Hebrew name for Simon Peter (John 1:42) and would have found a ready audience among the Jews in the Corinthian church. Still others chose Paul as their champion, and some even chose to identify with Christ (!).

"Has Christ been divided?" (1:13)—we can almost hear the sadness and exasperation in Paul's voice.[14] The problem was not in their baptism but in ascribing the importance of their identity to mere men rather than to Christ. In other words, the Corinthians were baptized *rightly* but began distinguishing or identifying themselves *wrongly*. Since *Christ* has not been divided, the *church of Corinth* had no right to be divided—especially over that which was supposed to unite them! In dividing into schisms or party names (i.e., denominations), they succumbed to a worldly mentality. It is *Christ* who gives their baptism meaning, not Paul, Apollos, or Cephas (Peter); they were baptized in the name of *Christ*, not anyone else (Acts 2:38).

In light of the Corinthians' divisions based upon who baptized them—and this is a critical point of the apostle's response—Paul is glad that he only baptized a handful of people (1:14–17).[15] ("Crispus" is undoubtedly the leader of the synagogue in Corinth [Acts 18:8]; "Gaius," a common name, may be the one mentioned in Rom. 16:23.) His statement, "For Christ did not send me to baptize, but to preach the gospel" (1:17), is hardly meant to nullify the need for baptism in the context of salvation.[16] Baptism (immersion) in water is essential for salvation ("baptism now saves you"— 1 Peter 3:21); it is impossible to be "clothed with Christ" (Gal. 3:27) or united with Christ (Rom. 6:3–4) otherwise. And yet, while many different men could baptize believers in water, few could reveal divine doctrine with apostolic authority. Thus, the apostle Paul gave personal priority to preaching the gospel over immersing people in water.[17] "Paul is by no means discrediting baptism. … [but] had to use all his time and talent to preach the Word and hence left the matter of baptism primarily to others."[18]

By exalting themselves according to petty divisions over men, the Corinthians were in danger of making the cross of Christ "void" or useless (1:17). They were willing to honor men at Christ's expense—something Paul would never do.

Questions

1.) Is "church of God" (1:1) as acceptable as "church of Christ" for designating a congregation of God's saints (1:2)? Are these formal names required by divine decree or merely *descriptors* that we can use interchangeably?

2.) For all the corrections and admonitions in this letter, Paul still begins by calling them "saints" (1:2) and refers to them throughout this letter as "brethren" (20 times). What does this tell us concerning:

   a.   Believers who are *ignorant* and *mistaken* yet still striving to serve Christ as Lord? (Does Christ still regard these people as Christians?)

   b.   Paul's expectations of those who are ignorant and mistaken? (Is he content to let them remain in this condition?)

   c.   Our own fellowship with such people? (If Paul recognized *his* fellowship with such people, then how should *we* regard them?)

3.) Does being of the "same mind" (1:10) require that *all* members of a given congregation agree on *every* issue, biblical topic, or spiritual subject? Or are there *some* topics that we *must* agree on, while others do not require unanimous agreement—and if so, *how do we know* which is which?

4.) What do you suppose prompted the Corinthians to call themselves after mere men rather than to identify only with Christ (1:11–12)? How might this same spirit of division still manifest itself within the brotherhood today? Please explain.

Lesson Two:

The Paradoxical Word of the Cross (1:18–31)

The "Foolishness" of the Gospel (1:18–25): The "word of the cross" (1:18) is synonymous with the gospel of Christ. This "word" includes not only the crucifixion but everything necessary to lead up to that event, all the implications of it, and everything gained by it. Christians everywhere ought to give their full attention to Christ and all that He accomplished on the cross. This message is central to God's plan of redemption and fulfills His "eternal purpose which He carried out in Christ Jesus our Lord" (Eph. 3:11).

Despite this, the unconverted world simply regards Jesus as another starry-eyed revolutionary who died as a pitiful martyr. Some people think that Jesus failed to be who He said He was and do what He promised to do. To the world, the message of a crucified Savior is pure nonsense. The pathetic, bloodied image of Jesus on a cross appears "foolish" in the sight of those who only see what they want to see and do not consider all the facts. Paul refers to such people as "perishing," which refers to their spiritual condition (2 Cor. 4:3–4, 2 Thess. 2:10, and 2 Peter 3:9). Jesus came to save people *from* perishing (John 3:16), yet every person who rejects Him remains "dead" in their sins (Eph. 2:1–3).

Paul describes a world of doomed people who do not *know* they are doomed—those who sneer at the idea of being "saved" when they are oblivious to the fact that they are *lost*. Thus, they fail to see the reality of their own hopeless condition even as they mock the One who came to rescue them *from* it. In contrast, the "word of the cross" has enlightened those "who are being saved [or, are saved]" (1:18b) as to their true condition and have responded in faith to the demands *of* that message. To these (Christians), Jesus' work on the cross was not a sign of weakness or foolishness but incomprehensible strength and transcendent wisdom. It takes nothing less than divine power to overcome death and everything the world threw at Him (Phil. 2:5–11).

The *real* fool in this huge, cosmic drama is not the Christ who died upon a cross in an ultimate act of self–sacrifice but the one who *mocks* that event (1:19).[19] Thus, "Where is the wise man ... ?" (1:20)—i.e., it was not that God's prophecy failed, or that Christ was made the fool, but God carried out a plan so great, so wonderful, and so *powerful* that all the wise men among the Jews *and* Gentiles never figured it out or saw it coming. "[T]he wisdom of the world" refers to the limited, self–serving, and hopeless way men reason concerning God, themselves, and the meaning of human life. Yet, God's concern is to save believers, not to satisfy the spiritually ignorant expectations of unbelievers (1 Tim. 2:3–6).

Nonetheless, in their self–gratifying desire for the supernatural, "Jews ask for signs" (1:22)—i.e., they refuse to believe that Jesus was the Messiah (Christ) unless He provided them with a "sign" *worthy of their approval and expectations*. Even though Jesus provided numerous miraculous signs of His divine nature (John 10:37–38), the Jews continued to ask for more (Mat. 12:38, Luke 11:16, and John 6:30). In response, Jesus called them "an evil and adulterous generation" (Mat. 12:39), since their requests revealed their contradictory and godless hearts.

"Greeks" (1:22) refers in the most general sense to non–Jews, or heathens, but more specifically it identifies the Greek scholars, philosophers, and rhetoricians who placed high value on their own wisdom and eloquence. Such men sought a "philosophic demonstration of Christianity"[20]—one that they could incorporate into their own pagan and idolatrous thinking (see Acts 17:16–21, for example). Instead, Paul presented Christ to them with historic facts, fulfilled prophecies, demonstrations of miraculous power, and irrefutable wisdom—things with which the so–called wisdom of the "Greeks" could not contend (e.g., Acts 6:8–10 and 9:19b–22). Such men were convinced that they could deliver humankind from its afflictions and limitations through human wisdom, but they had no means to overcome the problem of human *sin*. Thus, both Jews (who justified themselves through their heritage) and Gentiles (who worshiped human wisdom) found the "word of the cross" to be foolish and offensive.

Even so, Paul preached the crucified Christ as the core of God's plan of redemption, regardless of what Jews or Greeks thought of it (1:23).[21] The "called" (1:24) are those who have heard the gospel of Christ, responded with obedience, and (thus) saved from perishing (recall 1:9). God manifested His divine power and heavenly wisdom through weak elements: Christ opened the door to heaven—a humanly–impossible feat—with a wooden cross and three nails! It takes *divine strength* and *perfect knowledge* to bring about salvation through a ministry begun with a virgin birth, filled with heavenly truth and numerous miracles, and ending with a planned crucifixion and the resurrection from the dead. The sincere, humble heart will gladly accept this; the heart bent on self–preservation and human glory will reject it. Thus, what seems "weak" and "foolish" on God's part is superior to anything man has ever produced by his own power or through his own thinking. The "foolishness" and "weakness" of God (1:25) are not factual conclusions but are from the perspective of the unbeliever. People see God as foolish and weak who are clueless as to His divine nature and oblivious to all He has done to *save* us.

Our Boast Is in the Lord (1:26–31): "For consider your calling, brethren" (1:26)—i.e., the world does not find you (Corinthians) intelligent or sophisticated enough to be more enlightened than the rest. In fact, "Corinthian" was purposely a disparaging and contemptible label. Nonetheless, some Christians in Corinth boasted in themselves, flaunted their spiritual gifts, and esteemed themselves even above the apostle himself—even though it was he who brought them the message of Christ. Paul thus chastises their haughtiness and presumption; he reminds them that, as far as the world is concerned, they are a despised lot. Paradoxically, *they* are the "foolish," "weak things of the world," and "base things" that God uses to *shame* the wise (1:27–28). God did not choose the Christians at Corinth because they were important; rather, they became important only because God chose them. As it is with them, so it is with all Christians since God saves all of us the same way. Therefore, "no man may boast before God" (1:29) because of his human effort (Rom. 4:2–5).

"But by *His* doing you are in Christ Jesus" (1:30a, emphasis added)—this does not mean that the believer does *nothing.* God will not act with saving grace apart from human faith, and this faith must be proved through demonstrations of obedience. Yet, the power to forgive sins, overcome human inadequacy, and save souls belongs to God and Him alone. We could not know anything factually about God unless He had revealed it to us, and the fullest revelation we have received is through the incarnation of His Son (John 1:17). We have no room to boast in our own salvation since Christ has done the far more difficult work, including what is humanly impossible (1:30b). So then, Paul says, "Let him who boasts, boast in the LORD" (1:31, cited from Jer. 9:23–24).

Questions

1.) Paul says that God is "well–pleased through the foolishness of the message preached to save those who believe" (1:21). What exactly does this mean? What does it *not* mean?

2.) Jesus warned us not to become stumbling blocks to anyone (Mat. 18:7, Rom. 14:13). How then can God allow His gospel to be a stumbling block to the Jews—or anyone else (1:23)? (Consider Mat. 21:42–44, Rom. 9:32–33, and 1 Peter 2:8 in your answer.)

3.) Christ is the believer's "wisdom from God, and righteousness and sanctification, and redemption" (1:30). Why is it so important that Christians see Him in this way? What are the implications if a Christian were to *refuse* to acknowledge these things about Christ?

Lesson Three:

Reliance on the Spirit
Rather Than on Men
(2:1–16)

The Power of the Message (2:1–5): The Corinthians boasted in their knowledge about Christ, their status as Christians, and the miracles they were able to perform. Yet, they failed to realize that *all* of this was only because Christ gave them such gifts. In contrast to their arrogance, Paul's preaching did not rely on cultivated oratory skills or complicated human philosophy—things typically idolized by the Greek culture (2:1). Instead, he came to them in humility and with a simple message of "Jesus Christ, and Him crucified" (2:2).[22] A man crucified as though a vile criminal is not something that Greek philosophers would brag about or ever saw coming. Yet this was heaven's "testimony" to them—something they received from heaven (through Paul) but did not discover on their own.

Even so, Paul admits that "I was with you in weakness and in fear and in much trembling" (2:3)—probably because he feared physical harm due to his preaching (Acts 18:9–10), as he had received in previous cities (such as Lystra and Philippi; see Acts 14:19–20, 16:22–24). He did not possess the speaking skills of a Greek rhetorician, nor was this necessary; instead, he proclaimed a life–giving message of hope and backed his words with demonstrations "of the Spirit and of power" (2:4)—i.e., the miracles he performed among them (2 Cor. 12:12). While the Corinthians had divided themselves over who had baptized them (recall 1:13–17), they should have *stood together* in the unifying message of Christ. While they put great faith in men with great speaking abilities, Paul underscored his message with *miracles* so that "your faith would not rest on the wisdom of men, but on the power of God" (2:5; see Heb. 2:3–4).

The Mature Wisdom of Believers (2:6–16): Those among the Corinthians who are "mature" (2:6)—i.e., knowledgeable, wise, and discerning— accepted the message of Christ and Him crucified for what it was: a testimony from God Himself. Others, however, saw Christ as an opportunity for personal advancement, a reason to boast in what they knew, or even to flaunt their abilities to exercise spiritual gifts. But these latter Corinthians were not the first or the only men to have put overconfidence in the flesh. The Jewish authorities ("rulers") who conspired against Christ and sought His death also failed to see Christ for who He was (John 11:49–50, Mat. 27:20, Acts 3:17, 5:30, etc.). Their "passing away" refers not only to their eventual deaths, but implies that the conclusions they drew—namely, that Jesus was *not* the Christ—were among the false conclusions of this world. They should have recognized their own Messiah, since all the proof necessary to convince them was standing right in front of them. Instead, their reliance on their own wisdom blinded them to the Spirit's testimony among them (in the form of Jesus' teaching, miracles, and fulfillments of prophecy).

What had once been mysterious and obscure has now been disclosed and made clear. This mystery "now revealed" was all part of God's plan from long ago (see Eph. 3:1–12). Through the Law, then the prophets, then His Son, and finally His apostles, God had consistently and methodically unveiled His plan of redemption for the salvation of all those who would call upon His name for salvation (Acts 2:16–21, Rom. 10:11–13). If the Jews had rightly understood all of this, they never would have crucified the Son of God (2:8–9).[23]

"For to us God has revealed" these things (2:10)—"us" being (first) Christ's apostles, and then (second) the church. The source of our knowledge about God and His salvation did not come from men but came by way of revelation of His Spirit (Gal. 1:11–12). The Holy Spirit not only knows the thoughts and intentions of men (Heb. 4:12) but of God Himself. There is much about the Holy Spirit that we will never understand in this life, but we do know that He is an individual Personage of God with His own identity and function. One of these functions is to serve as an intercessor between God and men (Rom. 8:26–27), but also to reveal God's *will* to men (Luke 2:26, Eph. 3:5, 1 Tim. 4:1, 1 Peter 1:12, , etc.). We could not have known God's unrevealed "thoughts" any more than we could know a man's unspoken thoughts (2:11).

The gospel itself is an expression of the Mind of God, rightly personified by Christ Himself.[24] As we have received the Spirit, so we have received (the message from) the mind of God (2:12), and thus we can know precisely what God wants us to know. The apostles served as the human spokesmen for this message. "[C]ombining spiritual thoughts with spiritual words" (2:13) in the Greek is simply "spiritual with spiritual," the words "thoughts" and "words" supplied by the NASB translators. This means, among other things, that the Holy Spirit revealed the gospel to these men who, in turn, revealed it to the world. The record of this information (in the NT epistles) serves as instructions for Christ's church, and thus serve as the pattern for Christians to follow from that point forward.[25]

A "natural man" (2:14) is one who is unspiritual in his thoughts, and therefore is not seeking God *or* His truth.[26] His mind will not accept the Mind of God because his heart is *unprepared* to do so. This is not a matter of his being *unable* to accept such things but his *unwillingness* to do so (as with many who heard Christ's parables—Mat. 13:10–15).[27] In this passage, Paul thus contrasts the "spirit of the world" (2:12) and the "Spirit of God" (2:11): the two are not compatible but stand opposed to each other (Gal. 5:16–17).

A spiritual person, however, rightly discerns the difference between worldly thoughts and divine revelation, as well as the excellent *value* of this revelation (2:15). "All things," in this context, refers to those "things" under discussion, namely, the things which God has revealed through His Spirit, to His apostles, and finally to His church. Those who are outside of Christ cannot rightly judge God's people since their system of appraisal is based on an inferior and godless standard. Even so, God's people cannot explain God or salvation apart from what the gospel has revealed to them. "But we have the mind of Christ" (2:16)—the "we" here is likely with reference, as in 2:12, to the apostles. Those who have the mind of Christ will speak the words of the Spirit (see 1 Cor. 14:37–38).

Questions

1.) Paul wrote, "I determined to know nothing among you except Jesus Christ, and Him crucified" (2:2; see 15:1–4). This is the core of his message to the Corinthians.

    a. Is "Christ and Him crucified" the core of *our* preaching today? (Is it the core of your own congregation's preaching?) If not, then what *is* its core preaching?

    b. Does making Christ the central message of our preaching mean that we cannot talk about anything (or anyone) else?

2.) If God's gospel is infinitely greater than man's own knowledge (2:6–8), why do most people reject *His* wisdom in favor of accepting *human* wisdom? What makes God's wisdom so unpopular and human wisdom so attractive?

3.) What can we know *factually* about God, our souls, or anything in the spiritual world if He had not revealed these things to us (2:10–13)?

    a. How dependent does this make us upon the written record of this revelation (the Bible) for *all* that we know, believe, teach, and do as Christians?

    b. Given this, should we be telling God how He should do things, or should we "take care how [we] listen" (Luke 8:18) to what He has told us?

4.) Paul wrote, "But we have the mind of Christ" (2:16). Can we—*should* we—also have the mind of Christ? If not, why not? If so, what exactly does this mean?

Lesson Four:

Building on Christ, Not Mere Men (3:1–23)

Behaving Like "Mere Men" (3:1–8): Having provided some general information concerning God's wisdom, authority, and revelation, and the role of His spokesmen (the apostles), Paul now turns his attention back to the Corinthian's immature perspective. Because of the way they were acting—dividing over who baptized them, challenging Paul's authority, and (as we will see) misusing God's spiritual gifts—Paul says he had to treat them as *children* rather than mature men (3:1). "Milk" and "solid food" (3:2) illustrate their lack of training, discernment, and maturity (Heb. 5:11–14). Instead of walking in Christ as they ought (1 John 2:6), they were "walking" like worldly men still governed by self–serving human ambition rather than led by God's Spirit (3:3). The "jealousy and strife" among them—the carnal, unspiritual, and very short–sighted elements of human competition—was evidence enough of this.

Specifically, the Corinthians' division over which man baptized them was petty and uncalled for (3:4). "What then is Apollos? And what is Paul?" (3:5): rather than serve the servant, the Corinthians were to serve the Master (Mat. 23:8–11, John 13:13–16). Mere servants of God are not the source (or power) of godly increase and spiritual maturity, but God is (3:6–7). Men cannot enlighten other men beyond their own ability; a stream cannot rise above its source. Men can plant seeds, and then water and fertilize them, but it is *God* who gives life to seeds and brings them to mature plants. God is the One who deserves credit for creating life, sustaining life, and causing *growth* among the living. If those who labor for God "are one" (3:8)—united on one objective and serving the same Master—then to *divide* over such men makes no sense at all.

God's Field, God's Building (3:9–23): Paul, Apollos, and Cephas (recall 1:12) are merely God's fellow workers, but "you are God's field" (3:9)—referring to the entire church in Corinth. Paul likens himself to a farmer who plants seeds in a "field" and allows God to do His work. The anticipation of a good crop *is* conditioned, however, not only upon good seed (words of truth) but also good soil (humble hearts) (Mark 4:1–20).

Paul then switches metaphors (with the same application), likening himself to a "wise master builder" who "laid a foundation" capable of supporting a church perpetually (3:10).[28] He refers to the fact that he founded the church in Corinth, as it was part of his ministry to establish churches (Rom. 15:20–21); "and another is building on it" refers to teachers at Corinth who continue what he began. Such teachers have the serious responsibility to make sure that *what* they teach—and even *how* they teach it—agrees with the gospel revealed by God (James 3:1).

Paul openly reveals the foundation upon which the Corinthian church was built: Jesus Christ—the Man *and* His message (3:11). Just as a man who has not been "born of God" (John 1:12–13) poses falsely as a Christian, so a church that does not have Christ as its foundation masquerades as belonging to Him.

Now Paul shifts to what is built *upon* that foundation (3:12): just because the foundation is acceptable does not mean what others build upon it will be. In descending order (according to value), Paul lists several kinds of building materials, illustrating the different quality of teaching and preaching that various teachers might offer the church in Corinth. The different materials here—gold, silver, precious stones, etc.—are not different church doctrines, as some have supposed, but represent Christians of varying strengths (of faith) and virtues, especially as applied to a given congregation.[29] Some are able to endure fire, such as metals and stones; others are destroyed by fire, such as wood and straw (3:13). The "fire" here is probably any kind of "testing" (e.g., 1 Peter 1:6–9).

However, just because Paul laid a proper foundation does not guarantee that the Corinthians are building upon it rightly. Indeed, they *cannot* do so by acting in arrogance and with immaturity. One who *does* build successfully—by contributing to the health, growth, and perpetuation of the congregation—will receive a reward (3:14). One who unintentionally builds differently than what God intended "will suffer loss," but not necessarily the loss of his soul (3:15).

Paul seems to refer here to the immature or misguided efforts of an otherwise well-intentioned teacher. We should not label every misguided person a "false teacher." On the other hand, one who purposely *destroys* a congregation—a false teacher indeed—"God will destroy him" (3:16–17), since that person has shown no regard for that which is holy to God.[30] Paul says that the church in Corinth is like a temple of God—not the meeting place itself, but the collective membership of its believers—and no *human decision* ought to destroy a temple of *God*. This "temple" is holy because God's Spirit indwells it.

The attitudes and behaviors of worldly men will never lead to spiritual maturity and effective teaching; "Let no man deceive himself" into believing otherwise (3:18–20). To "become foolish," as Paul states here, means to choose that which seems foolish in the world's view (recall 1:23) but is in fact wisdom from God. The Lord knows that "the reasonings" of human wisdom cannot begin to address the problem of human sin.[31]

"For all things belong to you" (3:21–23) is Paul's way of saying: instead of lowering yourselves to the glory of men, you should see yourselves as heirs of all things *through Christ*. It is Christ who raises us up, not men; our boast is in Him, not in other men or even in ourselves. Since we belong to Christ, and Christ belongs to the Father, therefore we belong to the Father. Lipscomb paraphrases 1:21: "All that the men [who are] sent from God teach is the common heritage of all who believe in God. ... No revelation to man was for personal use, but for the good of all the children of God."[32]

Questions

1.) Paul called the Corinthians "infants in Christ" (3:1) even though many of them had been Christians for several years. This begs the question: does *time alone* create spiritual maturity? If so, then are *all* "seasoned" Christians wise and mature? If not, *what does*?

2.) Paul wrote, "I planted, Apollos watered, but God was causing the growth" (3:6). What should we expect such "growth" to look like? Are we to know *how* God causes such growth before we *can* grow? (Consider Mark 4:26–29 in your answer.)

3.) "The wisdom of this world is foolishness before God" (3:19). Likewise, Jesus said, " … That which is highly esteemed among men is detestable in the sight of God" (Luke 16:15). How should these principles affect how we practice:

    a. Marriage?

    b. Parenting?

    c. Finances (and other realms of stewardship)?

    d. Daily Christian living?

    e. Collective activity (as a congregation, or with other Christians generally)?

    f. Worship (individually or collectively)?

Lesson Five:

The Christian's Attitude toward God's Stewards (4:1–21)

Paul now turns his attention to the Corinthians' personal regard for him. There is obvious tension between a certain element within the Corinthian church and Paul, and he seeks to expose and then resolve this. (Unfortunately, this problem does not go away entirely, and he will need to address it more pointedly in a second letter.) Paul knows who he is and where he stands with the Lord; he has been commissioned to be an apostle (Acts 26:16–18) and the Corinthians should have shown due respect for this. He is Christ's servant who has the responsibility to reveal the "mysteries of God" to His people (4:1).[33] Obviously, God found Paul "trustworthy [or, faithful; dependable]" for this responsibility, regardless of what men thought of him.

Yet, certain men at Corinth see themselves on par with the apostle, if not even more knowledgeable or capable than him. Paul responds to this in three ways:

❑ **First (4:1–5):** "[I]t is a very small thing that I may be examined by you, or by any human court [or, judgment]" (4:3). This recalls the appraisal issue from 2:14–15: Paul is insinuating that his critics are not spiritually wise in their estimation of him and his work but are succumbing to the world's system of judging things. Paul's apostleship is not dependent upon the acceptance or approval of any people.

❑ **Second (4:6–13):** Paul was not exceeding "what is written"—a reference to the OT prophecies which Christ had fulfilled—but human arrogance *will* exceed this. Some Corinthians acted as though they did not need Paul any longer—or had *never* needed him, boasting that they "had not received" the gospel from him (4:7). They act like they have already arrived, even though their smug attitude displayed nothing more than spiritual immaturity (4:8).

Paul counters their presumptive boasting with the difficult and self-sacrificial life of an apostle (4:9–13). He had endured much loss and persecution to bring the gospel to the Corinthians; they had not suffered any of these things yet put themselves on the same level as (or even higher than) Paul. They wanted all the glory *of* an apostle (as they saw it) without having to serve or suffer *as* an apostle. In his own words, Paul describes the difficult and humiliating work of both him and his fellow apostles (4:9–10).

Paul then exposes the personal rigors of the apostleship—things he must endure to bring the gospel to men (4:11–13). He presents a sobering, graphic, and pathetic picture—and yet the bragging Corinthians have had to endure *none* of this.

❑ **Third (4:14–21):** Throughout this section, Paul is not speaking maliciously or spitefully. He simply wants the Corinthians to see how arrogant they sound to him—and to Christ. His words exhibit sadness and disappointment (as in Gal. 4:11). Yet, as their "father through the gospel" (4:15), he has a right to administer discipline as needed toward those who remain arrogant. In other words, if they are going to act like children, then he will bring the "rod" to them as a father would his son (4:21; see Prov. 13:24).

But this is not at all what Paul desires. Instead, he wants them to act with maturity, like himself; "be imitators of me" (4:16; 1 Cor. 11:1). He also has sent Timothy to help them to achieve this, since he (as a "kindred spirit"—see Phil. 2:19–22) knows exactly what Paul's expectations are. ("Timothy" is most likely the young man whom Paul converted in Lystra [Acts 16:1–3] and the recipient of the epistles we know as *1 & 2 Timothy*.) What Paul and Timothy teach to the Corinthians is the same as what they teach in "every church" (4:17)—a testimony to the unity and consistency of Paul's gospel.

In time, Paul himself will come to them; the nature of that visit will depend upon how the Corinthians receive his apostolic instruction. "For the kingdom of God does not consist in words but in power" (4:20)—

i.e., the Corinthians talked a big talk, but Paul has the backing of the King (Christ) to defend him.

With these thoughts, Paul wraps up his response to the divisions that are evident among the Corinthians—a discussion that began in 1:10. He has shown them how unnecessary, infantile, and counterproductive their divisions have been (and always *are* among God's people). But this is not just a "teaching moment" for Paul; he always warns of discipline and punishment if the Corinthians do not rectify this problem. In the following chapters, he will begin to address other problems within the Corinthian church to bring about their repentance and correction.

Questions

1.) Should we adopt Paul's view (4:3) regarding those who are critical of *us*?

    a.   Should we disregard all criticism simply because it *is* criticism (and especially when it is unfavorable to us)? Why or why not?

    b.   Given Paul's statement in 4:4, are we innocent before *God* if we find nothing wrong with *ourselves*? Please explain.

2.) What did Paul mean by "do not go on passing judgment before the time" (4:5)? (Consider Eccles. 7:8, Rom. 14:7–12, and James 4:11–12 in your answer.)

3.) How does 4:18–21 sound (in a sense) like Christ talking to the entire world—Christians and non–Christians alike?

Lesson Six:

Arrogance Corrupts Christian Fellowship (5:1–13)

Paul's Condemnation of the Corinthians' Arrogance (5:1–8): So far, Paul has been general in his comments about the Corinthians' less–than–desirable attitude. For the next few chapters, he will reveal other problems the Corinthians need to address and resolve, beginning with the most obvious one: their having allowed a man who has "his father's wife" to remain in their spiritual fellowship (5:1ff). The implication is that this man "has" this woman in wedlock, or possibly even outside of wedlock (i.e., in concubinage, or sexual fornication).[34] In any case, Paul refers to the union repeatedly as "immorality [or, fornication]."[35] Whether this "wife" was the man's biological mother or his stepmother is irrelevant; the fact that she was once the wife of his father makes this an incestuous relationship (a moral abomination; see Lev. 18:8, 20:11).[36] Non–Christian Gentiles thought little of illicit sex, but even they refrained from blatant incest.

The Corinthians' improper *toleration* of this situation is as sinful as the man's sin itself: their failure to condemn the man's sin made them accomplices to it. If the Corinthians were so wise and spiritually minded, Paul implies, they would have already removed this man from their fellowship. They should have grieved over this man's sin rather than given willful endorsement to it (5:2).

Since the Corinthians had refused to act, Paul must exercise his apostolic authority on the matter (5:3–5). "The swiftness of Paul's judgment stands in sharp contrast with the tardiness and toleration of the Corinthians."[37] "In the name of the Lord Jesus" (5:4) indicates a strong and binding judgment. To "deliver such a one to Satan" (5:5) meant that this man would no longer have the gracious providence of God (as Christians enjoy), and Satan would be given considerable influence over his life and health (1 Tim. 1:20 and 2 Thess. 2:10–11). This man is already under Satan's control; the congregation needs to step away from him so that they also will not be under

Satan's control.[38] This excommunication does *not* mean the man could not repent; in fact, Paul anticipates his repentance, and it is believed that 2 Cor. 2:6–11 is an appeal to his restoration. (On "the day of the Lord Jesus," see comments on 1:18.) However, it *does* mean his brethren would sever him from their company and fellowship unless he repented.

"Boasting" (5:6) indicates self–exaltation, which is always the objective of human pride. A small amount of boasting corrupts one's entire heart—in this case, even an entire congregation. "Leaven" indicates the introduction of an outside influence to produce fermentation, thus taking on a life of its own, so to speak (Gal. 5:9). Just as the ancient Hebrews were instructed to remove leaven from their kneading bowls in observance of the Passover (Exod. 12:19–20), so Christians must remove any "leaven" (i.e., boasting, human arrogance, man–made impositions, etc.) from among them in honor of Christ, our Passover Lamb (5:7). Thus, we are to "celebrate the feast" (5:8)—an allusion to the Lord's Supper but also a figurative implication of one's fellowship with God through Christ—with purity of heart.

The Focus of Church Discipling (5:9–13): "I wrote to you in my letter … " (5:9)—indicating a previous written correspondence no longer in existence. In that letter, Paul instructed the Corinthians "not to associate with immoral people," or not to engage in *spiritual fellowship* with such people. It is impossible to escape all association with the immoral and idolatrous people of the world. Paul's statement that we would have to go *out* of the world to avoid them is a purposely exaggerated way of saying, "The world is filled with them."

Even so, the godless behavior of the world must *never* be allowed among the brethren (5:10–11). A "so–called" brother is one who claims to be a friend of Christ but lives as a friend of the world, exhibiting behavior unbecoming of a Christian. Such a one makes himself an enemy of God (Rom. 8:5–9, James 4:4)—a serious offense. "[N]ot even to eat with such a one" (5:11b) is not in reference to the Lord's Supper (although it applies to that as well) but a common meal (see 2 John 1:10–11). In the ancient Orient, to sit down at a table together for a meal communicated *fellowship* between the participants of that meal; Paul says *nothing* must be done that communicates spiritual fellowship with one who has been *dis*–fellowshipped from his congregation.

The process of church discipline loses all its power when members of the congregation do not honor it (see Rom. 16:17, 2 Thess. 3:6, 14, and Titus 3:10).

We have no authority over those who are not in Christ ("outsiders"); even Paul does not level a judgment against them (5:12). God will deal with such people Himself. However, we do have the right and responsibility to "judge" (i.e., to render a verdict concerning sin) those *within* the church—particularly within our own congregation.[39] "Responsibility for [such] judgment is in the hands of the whole body of believers, not of a small group of ministerial authorities."[40] Such judgment (discernment) must be equitable, balanced, and exercised in love (Mat. 7:1–2, 2 Thess. 3:15, etc.) to keep the church pure. Thus, "Remove the wicked man from among yourselves" (5:13)—a godly injunction carried over from the Law of Moses regarding the purging of wicked men from among Israel (Deut. 13:5, 17:7, etc.).

Questions

1.) For what reasons—beyond arrogance itself (5:2)—might a congregation refuse to act quickly and decisively in response to sin within its membership?

2.) Many believe that dealing with sin in the camp (see Josh. 7 for the reference) is the responsibility of the leadership (shepherds) of a given congregation. Yet, who else needs to rectify this problem? (Consider 2 Cor. 2:5–7 and James 4:7–10 in your answer.)

3.) Why did Paul not implement the step–by–step instructions Jesus prescribed in Mat. 18:15–17? Does this mean that we do not always have to use those instructions? Was this a special case not defined *by* those instructions? Or … what do you think?

4.) Paul uses "immoral" (or "immorality") four times in this chapter. Besides having one's "father's wife," what are other manifestations of immorality to which Christians might easily succumb? If one will not repent of *these* immoralities, then is *he* a "wicked man" that ought to be removed from the congregation (5:13b)?

Lesson Seven:

Worldly Judgments against Christian Brethren (6:1–11)

The Uselessness of Lawsuits between Brethren (6:1–8): Paul now cites another example of the Corinthians' arrogance and spiritual immaturity: they are suing their own brethren in civil courts before secular judges. "Neighbor," in this context, must refer to a fellow Christian, not one's fellow man (6:1). Paul just finished saying (in 5:12) that we have no business judging those outside the body of Christ. And yet, it is shameful for spiritual brothers in Christ to allow worldly–minded men render legal judgments between them!

"Does any one of you … dare to go to law … ?" (6:1) does not mean that lawsuits of any kind are altogether forbidden but that lawsuits between Christians ought to be *unnecessary*. If saints will have the responsibility to "judge the world"[41]—in some future, otherworldly context—then most certainly they should be able to decide cases between *themselves* (6:2). He even says that we will "judge angels" (6:3)—most certainly a reference to what we call *fallen* angels (since there is no indication in Scripture that good angels, being innocent, will stand judgment for anything). Our decision to have followed Christ will condemn ("judge") *their* decision to have abandoned God: even though we had never seen God, but they saw Him in His glory (Mat. 18:10).

Instead of relying on secular judges, those who are "wise" within the congregation ought to settle disputes and resolve legal issues among Christians (6:4–6).[42] These wise men will likely be church elders but can be (or include) other men as well. (I say "men" here because there is no example in the NT of women rendering a decision for other Christians, and because Paul also cites a "wise man" here.) This follows the pattern of how the ancient Israelites used to plead their cases before the elders at the gates of their cities (e.g., Ruth 4:1–12, Job 29:7–17). The repeated "Or do you not know … ?" phrase seems a form of reproof, as in, "Since you are so wise—or so you claim—*you should know this already!*" The idea of brothers in Christ taking each other to court implies that believers are no better than unbelievers when it comes to settling our differences. It also implies that we have no "wise man" among us who can mediate such a dispute.

Paul says that this action "is already a defeat [or, defect; loss] for you" (6:7): in a useless attempt to solve one problem, a new one is created. It is therefore a dishonor to the Christian faith to behave this way. Paul says that it is better to suffer the loss (of whatever the litigation is trying to preserve or recover) than it is to battle it out in court. Or, it is "better [to] undergo wrong yourself than suffer defeat in the matter of love and forgiveness of a brother."[43] The injury this inflicts upon the brother being sued, not to mention the congregation's reputation, has far greater damage than whatever alleged damage the lawsuit itself sought to address.

Such acts of litigation imply the Corinthians' distrust that their own brothers in Christ would deal fairly with them. This is the silent accusation behind Paul's statement (6:8), "You yourselves wrong and defraud"—i.e., you imply that your own brethren are untrustworthy, are incapable of rendering justice, or seek your harm. Not only this, but they exhibited distrust or impatience in God's exercise of justice over all men through their failure to bring the matter before Him. In effect, the Corinthian reasoned, "Since I do not believe I will get a fair hearing before my own brethren, and I cannot wait for God to vindicate me, I must have the courts of law solve this dispute between me and my fellow Christian."

Two Very Different Groups (6:9–11): Bringing Christians' lawsuits before worldly judges implies that there is no (spiritual) difference between the two groups. The apostle Paul sharply disagrees: the "unrighteous" have nothing in common with those who belong to Christ (see 2 Cor. 6:14–18). "Do not be deceived" (6:9)—i.e., do not accept this false line of reasoning. The numerous warnings in the NT against being deceived (1 Cor. 3:18, 15:33, Gal. 6:3, 7, Eph. 5:6, etc.) indicate just how common deception really is and how easy it is to succumb to it. Since the "unrighteous … will not inherit the kingdom of God," it is pointless to turn to their counsel for those things which *saints* ought to be able to handle themselves.[44] Paul gives examples of such people who will not inherit the kingdom of God. This list is not meant to be comprehensive, and implies *active lifestyles*, not incidental occurrences of sin.

- ❏ **"fornicators"**: those who freely engage in sexual activity outside of marriage, as described in the next section (6:12–18).[45] It refers generally to any illicit sexual relations.
- ❏ **"idolators"**: or image–worshipers, but this can be used literally or figuratively.[46] For example, a man viewing pornography is an image worshiper, but so is a woman whose devotion to her children or grandchildren is put ahead of her devotion to God. Both are worshiping the *creation* over the *Creator* (Rom. 1:25).
- ❏ **"adulterers"**: specifically, *covenant–breakers*, since "adultery" necessitates the violation of a covenant, whether one's own or someone else's. Illicit sex outside of marriage is fornication; illicit sex involving a married person is adultery. While adultery can also have a figurative meaning regarding the violation of one's covenant with God (James 4:4), Paul has in mind here sexual adultery.
- ❏ **"effeminate"**: This word means "soft" (as in Mat. 11:8 and Luke 7:25), but here the word has to do with being "luxurious and dainty," especially of men who are acting and dressing like women.[47] The Greek word here [*malakoi*], in this context, "literally means those who are soft and effeminate; those who have lost their manhood and who live for the luxuries of recondite [i.e., difficult to understand] pleasures … ."[48]
- ❏ **"homosexuals"**: The KJV renders this "abusers of themselves with mankind." The Greek word here [*arsenokoites*] refers to a sodomite, a man who abuses and thus defiles himself sexually with another man (which was the darkest sin of Sodom; see Gen. 19:1–11 and Jude 1:7). Paul expounds upon this explicitly in Rom. 1:24–28, where he refers to such behavior as a "dishonor," "a lie," "unnatural," "indecent," and an "error," being the result of "a depraved mind."[49]
- ❏ **"thieves"**: a general term referring to anyone who steals time, money, material goods, property, or anything else.[50]
- ❏ **"covetous"**: while thievery has to do with taking something that does not belong to you (Exod. 20:15), coveting has to do with an *evil desire* for this same thing (Exod. 20:17; see Rom. 7:7–8). It is an act of the heart, not of the hand and is a form of idolatry or greed (Eph. 5:5).
- ❏ **"drunkards"**: this refers to those overcome with alcohol, especially as

a lifestyle or addiction (Rom. 13:13, Gal. 5:21, 1 Tim. 3:3, Titus 2:3, 1 Peter 4:3, etc.).

- ❑ **"revilers":** Paul refers here to one who speaks abusively against someone or something else that deserves respect; technically, one who is a mischief–maker with his speech.[51]
- ❑ **"swindlers":** the Greek word here [*harpax*] has to do with snatching away something from someone by force, as in Mat. 11:12, 13:19 and John 10:12.[52] In a general sense, it refers to any kind of extortion, cheating, or conning someone out of what is rightfully theirs.

"Such were some of you" (6:11)—i.e., Paul was not speaking hypothetically but factually about what he originally encountered among the Corinthians. They were people with whom many of us today would choose to avoid having any contact. Yet they were "washed," "sanctified," and "justified" to be set apart from worldly behavior, no longer to identify with it. "Washed" refers to one's baptism (immersion) in water for the purpose of becoming a Christian (Acts 2:38, Rom. 6:3–7, Gal. 3:26–27, etc.). "Sanctified" refers to (the act of) becoming a *saint*, or one made holy to God (recall 1:2, 30). "Justified" is a legal term synonymous with being made innocent (or just) before God. "[I]n the name of the Lord Jesus Christ" indicates the *authority* by which the Corinthians were justified; "in the Spirit of our God" indicates the *means* by or *context* in which this was accomplished.

Questions

1.) Paul said "it is already a defeat" for two Christians to bring their legal dispute before a secular court of law (6:7). Why is this? Does this mean that we should overlook justice in any case that involves two Christians? Please explain.

2.) Paul also wrote (6:7), "Why not rather be wronged? Why not rather be defrauded?" What does he mean by these statements? Are you to let a fellow Christian get away with taking advantage of you, your property, or your kindness?

3.) Paul was very explicit on who *will not* inherit the kingdom of God (6:9–10).

   a.   But who *will* inherit it—and how do we know this?

   b.   Is God's *denying* salvation to anyone a violation of His *love* for that person?

Lesson Eight:

The Christian Belongs to the Lord
(6:12–20)

"Lawful" Does Not Always Mean "Profitable" (6:12–14):** "All things are lawful for me" (6:12a)—Paul does not mean that anything is *permissible* (for he has just mentioned several behaviors that are indeed *unlawful*). Just because something is *doable* does not mean it is "profitable [or, expedient]." Going to court is not wrong in itself; taking your *brother* to court out of greed, distrust, spite, vengeance, etc. *is* wrong. Likewise, sex is not wrong in itself; illicit sexual relations (fornications) *is* wrong. Whatever is profitable must seek the will of God; whatever God says is good is also "profitable" (2 Tim. 3:16–17). Certain *conditions* must be met for something to be considered profitable (see 1 Cor. 10:23).

"I will not be mastered by anything" (6:12b)—i.e., I will not let what *can* be done to dictate what I *will* do. The mere possibility of an action does not determine its worthiness or legitimacy (1 Cor. 7:23, 9:27). There is nothing abnormal with an *appetite* for the things of the world, but we are to exercise discretion, restraint, and even self–denial toward these things (6:13). "All appetites, passions, and lusts are for our good, if properly used and restrained. If they enslave us, they degrade and destroy us."[53] Indulging in *temporary* things (such as food) at the expense of *eternal* things is pointless and hopeless. The Christian's physical body is to be used in pursuit of spiritual life; God did not give us a body to engage in sin (immorality) but to serve Him (Rom. 6:12–13). Paul even takes it a step further (6:14): just as *Christ's body* was raised from the dead, so will *our body* (Phil 3:20–21).[54] Thus, we should use our body in service to God with a view to its resurrection from the dead.

The Christian's Body Belongs to the Lord (6:15–20): Even though our body dies, it will still be associated *in some future time* with glory. Therefore, we are not to use that same body for something unholy. Just as Christ would never join His own body to a prostitute (harlot), so Christ's *people* must

35

never do this (6:15). A sexual union with a prostitute—or any person who is not one's own spouse—makes a mockery of the natural order of Creation since God intended sexual relations between a man and a woman only in the holy union of marriage (6:16; Gen. 2:24). Since sexual immorality is not of God, it cannot create a legitimate marriage but an unholy (or wicked) union (compare Mat. 19:4–6).

Paul's strong words to the Corinthians are necessary since they are immersed in a society which indulges in fornication and other moral indiscretions. While Christians today may regard sin as a mere theological concept, this passage is gritty and real: since one's physical body belongs to God, what he does in his physical body must honor Him.[55] We cannot separate what we (claim to) believe in our hearts with what we do with our bodies. No other sin so flagrantly violates the Lord's possession of the Christian's body than when he gives that body to another in fornication (6:18; see 1 Thess. 4:3).

"But one who joins himself to the Lord is one spirit with Him" (6:17). Being "one spirit" with someone does not make you that person; it does not imply *equality* of identity or authority but *unity* of purpose and intention. Jesus claimed to be "one" with the Father (John 10:30); this did not *make* Him the Father but indicated His complete cooperation with the Father's will (as expressed in John 17:21–22). If one's will is wholly submitted to Christ's, then he must "flee immorality" and all other sins since these contradict his unity with the Spirit (6:18). Exactly *how* "the immoral man sins against his own body" in a way differently than all other sins is difficult to understand, but the emphasis here has to do with rendering oneself unfit for holy service. Simply put: the believer cannot be joined (in a holy union) with Christ *and at the same time* be joined (in an unholy union) with anyone or anything else (2 Cor. 6:14–16). This is because (6:19–20):

❏ **"your body is a temple of the Holy Spirit."** This cannot mean that the Holy Spirit is literally dwelling somewhere in one's physical body. It means that we are to give the Spirit authority *over* our physical body, to use it for His will, even as we have given our heart to Him for this same purpose. The Spirit's indwelling is like the human spirit's indwelling: not in some tangible, visible form, yet in a very real and demonstrable way (Rom. 8:9–11).[56]

- ❑ **"you are not your own."** If we are "in Christ," then He *owns* us (Rom. 6:11–13, Titus 2:14, and 1 Peter 2:9–10). Therefore, we have no authority to take that (our body) which belongs to another (Christ) and use it for any illegitimate purpose (sin of any kind).
- ❑ **"for you have been bought with a price."** The "price" of the purchase of our souls (which includes that which our souls animate—our bodies) is the blood of Christ, a payment of infinite, incalculable worth (1 Peter 1:18–19). Our objective, then, is to glorify God who is *in* our bodies (through the indwelling of His Spirit) *with* our bodies (in obedient service; Rom. 6:19).[57]

Questions

1.) Self–control, self–discipline, and self–mastery are regular themes in the NT concerning the Christian lifestyle (6:12). If we are not in control of ourselves, then does this necessarily imply that something (or someone) *else* is in control of us? If so, will this help us or harm us? Please explain.

2.) *Food* is for the stomach, but the *body* is not for immorality (6:13). God created food, the stomach, and the human body; but man "created" immorality through abusing that which God had made. What other sinful practices have people created that God never did?

3.) Does joining oneself to a prostitute make a man "one flesh" with her (6:16) in the same way that a man and woman are made "one flesh" in marriage (Gen. 2:24, Eph. 5:31)? Does an act of fornication create a holy union that is recognized by God (Mat. 19:6)?

4.) How should the idea of our physical bodies serving as a *temple of the Holy Spirit* (6:19) affect a Christian's view on the following:

   a. Modesty (dress)?
   b. Piercings (especially, those which visibly alter one's personal appearance)?
   c. Tattoos (especially, those which visibly alter one's personal appearance)?
   d. Extreme sports (or any elective dangerous activity)?
   e. Obesity (particularly due to lifestyle choices)?
   f. Smoking (including vaping, marijuana, and pipes)?

Lesson Nine:

Concerning Marriage
(7:1–16)

Marriage as a Safeguard against Immoralities (7:1–7): It is evident that the Corinthians had engaged in written correspondence with Paul concerning the subject of marriage and sexual propriety (7:1). It is possible that they had a debate among themselves: some maintained that marriage is necessary to be righteous to God; others claimed that God wants Christians to remain (or even *become*) single, arguing that *any* union with a spouse undermines his or her union with Christ. Paul immediately dispels the first argument: "it is good for a man not to touch a woman"—where "touch a woman" is a specific euphemism for sexual intercourse (see Exod. 19:15) but can also be a general euphemism for marriage. In other words, abstaining from marriage is "good" in the sight of the Lord but only if one can constrain his sexual desires and live in celibacy (Mat. 19:12).

"But because of immoralities … " (7:2)—i.e., if one is unable to constrain his carnal desires, causing him to pursue sexual fornication ("immoralities"), then he ought to get married. This *also* is good [implied], since God gave us marriage as a gift to provide us with a safe, clean, and righteous context in which to engage in sexual relations. To "have" one's spouse indicates sexual exclusivity, as is fitting in the covenant of marriage.

Sexual intercourse in marriage is described here as a conjugal "duty" that a husband and wife render to each other (7:3). This is not to reduce sex itself to a mere dutiful obligation but highlights the *moral responsibility* each spouse has to his wife or to her husband. Spouses of a given marriage have *authority* over each other in this regard (7:4); "Conjugal rights are equal and reciprocal."[58] Since a married couple is "one flesh" through the covenant of marriage (Eph. 5:31), the spouse no longer has exclusive claim to his (or her) own body but has pledged this to his mate.

Given this, the wife or husband does not have authority to intentionally or spitefully "deprive" the other of sex (7:5). The only exception for this is "by agreement for a time"—i.e., with mutual consent, and for a brief duration—*and* through devotion to prayer. The objective of this limited separation is to resolve differences between the spouses and/or to allow them to draw near to God through a kind of "fasting" from sexual intercourse. If it is for selfish reasons, or if it continues for too long, then each spouse may be tempted to pursue sexual satisfaction elsewhere; thus, they are to "come together again" to avoid giving in to satanic desires.

Such separation is "by way of [Paul's] concession, not of [God's] command" (7:6, bracketed words added; compare 7:31). Paul's personal desire is that Christians who can forego marriage altogether would do so. He considered his ability to live without a wife (i.e., without need of sexual gratification) as a "gift" from the Lord, so that he might be completely devoted to Him (7:32–34). He conceded that not everyone possesses this "gift" but may have a different one (7:7; see Rom. 12:6–8 and 1 Peter 4:10–11).

Instructions to Believers Who Are Married (7:8–14): "But I say to the unmarried and to widows" (7:8)—"I say" indicates Paul's apostolic advice, not legal requirements of the gospel. He is not prevented from being married (see 9:5) but has chosen to forego this in his service to God. But if one is unable to live alone (i.e., in celibacy), then Paul's apostolic advice is to get married (7:9).[59] "[B]urn {with passion}"—the words "with passion" being supplied by NASB translators, not the original Greek text—does not mean "burn *in hell*" but refers to raging sexual desires.

The next set of instructions (7:10–11) comes from the Lord (as a command) and is not merely Paul's personal advice. In the rest of this chapter, he mentions four different statuses:

- ❑ **Married**—regardless of whether this union involves believers or unbelievers (Paul addresses both scenarios separately). However, Paul always implies that at least *one* of the spouses is a believer and therefore speaks to this person.
- ❑ **Unmarried**—generally-speaking, anyone who is not presently bound by marriage (see 7:27, 32, 39). This can include virgins and widows, but

since Paul identifies these two groups specifically, he has in mind those who *were* married but are *now* divorced.[60]

❏ **Widows**—those who were legitimately married but whose spouses have died.

❏ **Virgins**—not merely "unmarried" but who have *never* married (as in Lev. 21:13–14 and Mat. 25:1ff); i.e., maidens, or never–yet–married daughters.

The first use of "married" here (7:10–11) *must* only refer to Christians, for Paul addresses "the rest" in the following section (7:12–16). This instruction is clear: "the wife should not leave her husband" and "the husband should not divorce his wife." Not only *can* one continue in marriage in service to the Lord but that this is His command.[61] Paul uses "leave" and "divorce" interchangeably because the result is the same: the termination of the marriage union.[62]

The wife is not to be faithless to her marriage vows by separating herself from her husband; the husband is not to send his wife permanently away—effectively creating a divorce—since "God hates divorce" (Mal. 2:16) and "from the beginning" this was never His plan (Mat. 19:4–6). This means that God defines the covenant of marriage in the Law of Moses the same as He does in the gospel of Christ. *Moral teachings* of marriage are constant and unchanging; conditions can change but morality never does.[63]

Paul includes a parenthetical phrase here (7:11): "but if she does leave"—meaning that a Christian wife *can* leave her Christian husband, yet this speaks to what is possible, not what is wise, expected, or pleasing to God.[64] Paul has already stated what pleases God: *stay married*. Even so, some Christian spouses will find themselves in what they believe to be a desperate, unworkable, and/or irreconcilable situation. "[I]f she does leave" can only be rectified by one of two scenarios: she must remain "unmarried" (i.e., having divorced her Christian husband, she no longer has permission to marry again), or she can be reconciled to her husband (if she has not already divorced him and he has married someone else).[65]

The Options of a Christian Who is Married to Another Christian:		
Remain faithfully married to your spouse	**SINCE**	this is what God intended "from the beginning" (Mat. 19:4–6).
Temporarily suspend sexual relations to pray and seek reconciliation with your spouse	**SINCE**	Paul allows this as a concession (7:5), but it is an atypical situation.
Leave the marriage temporarily	**BUT**	be reconciled to your spouse.[66]
Leave the marriage permanently	**AND**	in doing so, relinquish all rights to seek a different marriage.[67]

It must be understood that, even with these instructions, Paul does not address every possible situation. Extreme marital circumstances (physical abuse, chronic substance abuse, sexual deviancy, etc.) can and do exist which must be dealt with specially and individually. "What Paul writes still leaves a number of questions unanswered for us who are living under different circumstances. The best we can do is to absorb fully what the Lord and his apostle say and then to answer such additional questions in the light of their words and in their spirit."[68]

"But to the rest I say, not the Lord ... " (7:12)—the "rest" refers to mixed marriages of believers with unbelievers. Again, Paul clarifies that this is his apostolic advice, not revealed doctrine. Christians who are married to unbelievers are not to sever their marriages. Some reasons for this are addressed here:

❑ Marriage between a man and a woman is a sacred union even if it is not a union of two Christians. Failure to honor this union does not support one's claim to honor "what God has joined together."
❑ A Christian spouse can have a persuasive effect on her (or his) unbelieving spouse, so that he might obey the Lord (7:16), which is what Peter also says (1 Peter 3:1–2).
❑ The unbelieving spouse of this mixed union is "sanctified." This does not mean he (or she) is automatically *saved*. We are saved by grace

and through personal faith (Eph. 2:8), not through marriage or by association. Rather, Paul means that the presence of a Christian spouse *legitimizes* and provides a godly *influence for* that family's relationship.[69]

- ❑ "[F]or otherwise your children are unclean, but now they are holy"— this alludes to a ritual cleanness (or uncleanness) under the OT Levitical system. In that context, "unclean" did not necessarily mean sinful but simply unfit to come into God's presence (through the holy assembly of Israel). Paul seems to say that the presence of a godly spouse in the family allows for God's providence—in a sense, His presence—to govern and influence it.

If an "Unbelieving Spouse" Leaves (7:15): But if the unbelieving spouse leaves, this presents a different story (7:15). To "leave" must mean, in this context, to divorce (as in 7:10). In this case, "the brother or sister is not under bondage"—Paul speaks only to the Christian spouse, not the unbelieving one. "Bondage" indicates an enslavement or servitude; yet the question here is: to *what exactly* does the "bondage" refer? We may never resolve this question to everyone's satisfaction. The way Paul uses the word "bound" later (7:27, 39) indicates the binding of a man and a woman in marriage. (The Greek *words* are not identical, but their *usage* is consistent.) It is impossible for a marriage to exist or function with just one person (Rom. 7:1–2); thus, it is impossible for one to be "bound" to a marriage from which someone else has been *freed*, regardless of the reason. God has called us to live in peace, not in perpetual limbo, in turmoil, or to an obligation that is impossible to uphold.

Thus, Paul gives his opinion on the matter: *in the case of an unbeliever abandoning the marriage*, the believer is legally freed from that relationship. He becomes "unmarried," since he is no longer bound to a wife (and so with a wife and her husband). Likewise, *in such a case*, the believing spouse must not leave *God* to pursue his or her spouse. In effect, Paul is saying that the preservation of one's relationship with God is *more important* than the preservation of one's marriage (consider Luke 14:26). People were not made for marriage (i.e., to be enslaved to it or by it) but marriage was made for people (i.e., to provide a context for procreation and family according to the natural order of Creation) (Mark 2:27, in principle).

Questions

1.) Paul permitted limited cessation of sex between spouses "so that you may devote yourselves to prayer" (7:5). What do you suppose the purpose of their prayers ought to be? Does this passage give permission for couples to "separate" in the contemporary sense—i.e., to live apart from each other with separate lives and separate finances? Please explain.

2.) Paul's message to the Corinthians is: *stay married,* no matter who it is you are married to (i.e., believer or non–believer). Why is he so adamant about this?

   a. Should this be our instruction to married couples as well?

   b. In a passage where he had every opportunity to do so, why does Paul not question whether anyone who is now married has had a *previous* marriage?

3.) Is this section (7:1–16) meant to be a comprehensive treatise on marriage?

   a. If so, why are some critical questions left unaddressed—e.g., cases of infidelity, cases of spousal abuse, eligibility for marriage in the case of divorce, alcohol or substance addiction, and exceptional cases of all kinds?

   b. If not, why not? Are we not faced with the above situations?

   c. What should we do in situations involving problems of marriage or divorce where the Bible has not specifically spoken?

Lesson Ten:

Advice to Those Contemplating Marriage or Divorce (7:17–40)

The Condition in Which One Is Called (7:17–24): Paul begins this next section (7:17–24) with a general principle: *as* one is called (into Christ), *so* he can continue. This refers to one's marital status, as already discussed, but also extends to one's social standing (as a slave or freedman), his identity (as one circumcised or uncircumcised), his economic status (as rich or poor), or any parallel situation. Just because one becomes a Christian *does not mean* that his other statuses must necessarily change or be dissolved; the Christian lifestyle is able to accommodate many of them.[70] A Christian's "walk" with God is not affected by his social standing; therefore, changing or improving his status does not improve his walk with God (7:20). Paul's teaching on this matter is consistent (7:17; recall 4:17; see 11:16 and 14:33). Some specific points:

❑ Circumcision (7:18–19) was required by some Jews of Gentile believers (see Acts 15:1, 5, and Gal. 6:12–13). But Paul says no man must be circumcised to become a Christian (see Gal. 5:6, 6:15, and Col. 3:11).

❑ Slavery (7:21–23) in the ancient world was common; likely some Corinthian believers were slaves. Such people may wonder whether they should seek freedom from their enslavement to become servants of Christ. Paul sets the matter straight: "Do not worry about it [or, care not for it]" (7:21)—i.e., God does not require this, so you should not let it be a concern for yourself. At the same time, if one *can* obtain his freedom from slavery, "rather do that." Paul is careful *not* to portray Christianity as an excuse for widespread slave revolt.[71] "You were bought with a price" (7:23)—namely, the priceless blood of Christ (recall 6:19–20)—and so no man has the right to bind upon a believer more than what God requires of him.

❑ To emphasize his point, Paul repeats himself: compare 7:20 and 7:24. To "remain" is not a commandment but a guiding principle. Again, one's station in life, if it is not immoral, does not have to change to walk in fellowship with God.

Instructions for Believers Who Are Unmarried (7:25–40): In this
section, Paul gives advice for "virgins" contemplating marriage.[72] We should
not underestimate Paul's educated and enlightened opinion; even so, we
must read his comments in the *historical context* of when he wrote them. He
obviously knows difficult times are ahead, and this knowledge influences the
advice he offers. Consider some of his statements, both in *1 Corinthians* and
elsewhere:

❑ "in view of the present distress" (7:26) refers to social or economic
hardships that are already affecting the Corinthian Christians.
❑ "yet such [married couples] will have trouble in this life, and I am trying
to spare you" (7:28, bracketed words are mine)—this "trouble" likely
refers to the difficulty of discipleship to Christ, not the usual difficulties
encountered in marriage itself.
❑ "but … shortened" (7:29a)—Paul anticipates a distress for Christians
everywhere, as intolerance for the Christian faith grows from passive
disbelief to active persecution.
❑ "from now on both those who have wives should be as though they had
none," etc. (7:29b–31a)—in other words, *things are changing*, and this
change will cause distress for married and unmarried Christians alike.
❑ "for the form of this world is passing away" (7:31b)—indicating that the
ancient world's attitude toward Christianity will change for the worse.
The imperial-driven Roman persecutions of the church in the first and
second centuries would easily fulfill Paul's brief predictions here.

Paul recommended against marriage only due to the extraordinary hardships
that Christian couples will soon face. (This advice was only for those who
can accept remaining single; for those who could not, he recommends
marriage.) But he also advised against marriage from a practical point of
view: one who is married will divide his attention between his spouse
and the Lord (7:32–35). If one remains unmarried, however, then he (or
she) will "be holy both in body and spirit" (7:34)—i.e., given to the Lord,
without anyone else having authority over his heart *or* his body (recall
7:3–4).[73]

To be clear: marriage is a gift of God and therefore a *good* thing. Elsewhere,

Paul advocates marriage and a spouse's devotion to it (Eph. 5:22ff, 1 Tim. 5:14, and Titus 2:4–5). Thus, Paul is not negative toward marriage or trying to *prevent* people from getting married. Rather, he is promoting "what is appropriate [or, seemly] and to secure undistracted devotion to the Lord" *given what is about to come upon the church* (7:35). It is the historical, big-picture perspective that is driving his opinion here.

Next, Paul gives advice to fathers concerning their virgin daughters (7:36–38). "Virgin {daughter}" here can only refer to a daughter who still lives under her father's roof and thus is still under his authority. In the ancient world, it was disgraceful for a virgin girl of marrying age not to be married; it implied that there was something wrong—as in disgraceful or defective—with her or her family. A father reading Paul's earlier comments on *refraining* from marriage might take the apostle to mean that he (the father) was *sinning* by allowing his daughter to marry. Paul responds: "he does not sin; let her marry" (7:36) if that is what he believes is best for her, especially if she is unable to live in an unmarried state without succumbing to sexual sins.

On the other hand, Paul adds that there is nothing shameful or unbecoming to God if the father *refuses* to let his virgin daughter marry, if others are not compelling him to do this (7:37; recall 7:23). This refers to a father who "stands firm in his heart" that, for the protection and benefit of his daughter, he should refuse to give her away in marriage. This speaks of a situation "when there is no engagement, or contract, made in childhood, or promise made in early life that would bind him."[74]

Finally, Paul turns his attention to widows (7:39–40) and gives his apostolic advice concerning them. "A wife is bound as long as her husband lives" (7:39)—this is to be taken as a general statement (similar to Rom. 7:1–3), since in fact there are occasions when a wife is *no longer* bound to her husband even though he is not dead (1 Cor. 7:11, 15).[75] As much as God hates divorce (Mal. 2:16) and Christian leadership discourages divorce *and* encourages marriage, divorce *is* possible, and even God recognizes it when it happens (e.g., John 4:16–18). Again, it is legally, logically, and even biblically impossible for someone to be "bound" to a marriage when his or her spouse has been *freed* from it. If one is freed, then the marriage ceases to exist, and divorce is the result.

Thus, Paul's words ("A wife is bound as long as her husband lives") must be taken generally and not absolutely. The subject here is *widows*—women whose husbands have died. What *made* a woman a wife was her husband; upon his death, their marriage also died, in a sense, and she is no longer a wife but simply an unmarried woman. Thus, she is "free to be married" once released from the covenantal obligations of her former marriage. Paul states his own opinion on this: he submits that widows will be "happier" if they devote themselves to the Lord rather than seek another husband (7:40; see 1 Tim. 5:3–16). However, this does not have to be the case and she can marry another man if she so chooses. "[O]nly in the Lord" (7:39) is an expression which has no other natural reference except to another Christian (the *reasoning* for this may be found in 2 Cor 6:14–16).[76]

Questions

1.) When Paul says that "each man must remain in that condition in which he was called" (7:20), does that mean that it is a sin to *change* that condition? How do you know this, one way or the other?

2.) Do Christians today try to make "slaves" of other Christians (7:23)—over marriage, divorce, and other biblical subjects? If so, what exactly does this mean?

3.) Paul says candidly that when Christians get married, their interests will be divided (7:32–35). Anyone who has a healthy marriage can vouch for this.

   a. Does this portray marriage negatively—as something to avoid, if possible?

   b. Are we supposed to *choose* between a fulfilling marriage and serving as a faithful Christian, or is it entirely possible to pursue both and still be pleasing to God?

   c. On the other hand, please read Mat. 10:34–37 and Luke 14:26. What does Jesus require of *all* disciples, married or not?

Lesson Eleven:

The Proper Application of Christian Knowledge (8:1–13)

Knowledge Exercised with Love (8:1–3): "Now concerning things sacrificed to idols" indicates a new subject. The "things" here refers particularly to meats but can refer to other commodities as well. In Paul's day, *most* of the meat supply among the Gentiles was dedicated to one idol or another. Some of this meat was consumed within the pagan temples themselves, while the rest was sold in the marketplaces.

The objection to eating this meat, whether in a temple or at home, is based on the belief that doing so gives endorsement to idolatry—and even *participates* in it.[77] On the other side of the argument is the belief that, since idols are man–made gods, there is no harm in eating meat sacrificed to them. The problem Paul addresses (8:1–3) is not simply about whether to eat or not eat meat, but whether a Christian who holds to the second view will deal with his brother who holds the first view *in Christian love*. Just because one knows that idols are imaginary gods does not mean he will act in love toward his brother who sees things differently.

However, not *all* knowledge makes arrogant; not everyone who is knowledgeable is automatically arrogant; and not everyone who is arrogant is automatically knowledgeable. Paul is obviously making a statement based upon the situation he is confronting, not one concerning *all* knowledge in *every* context. Having knowledge *by itself* does not secure a man's righteousness before God, especially if he fails to show love to his brother in the process (1 John 4:8). Some have a better understanding of idols ("we know") than do others—and it is not a crime in either case. If a Christian boasts in what he *knows*, he has not yet learned how to *exercise* that knowledge in a proper way ("as he ought"—8:2). In contrast (8:3), one's genuine love for God will lead him to treat his less–than–knowledgeable brother in the Lord with godly love, respect, and dignity. Because of his knowledge *and* love, and his fellowship with God, he will be approved (or "known") by Him (2 Cor. 10:18, 1 John 3:23–24).

Affirmation of the One True God (8:4–6): Paul knew—and so did many of the Corinthians ("we know")—that an idol is nothing, and the god that it represents is also nothing (8:4–5; see Acts 17:24–28). There is only one *genuine* God, and He has sovereign authority over all that He has created. Paul *does*, however, acknowledge that many "gods" and "lords" do in fact exist, but only in the minds of their worshipers and in the public imagination. Unlike God ("from whom are all things"), they have no life and no power to do anything (see Psalm 115:4–8).[78] On a practical level, it is not a moral crime to eat meat sacrificed to a god that does not exist.

"[Y]et for us there is one God, the Father … " (8:6)—"us" meaning Christians in general, for this is a doctrinal statement of our belief (Eph. 4:6). Our God is not only alive but is the Giver of life, the center of all of Creation, and the Father of all spirits (Heb. 12:9). None of this can be said of any man–made idol or its god. "[A]nd one Lord, Jesus Christ … " (8:6)— Paul differentiates between God the *Father* and Christ the *Son*, who serves as our Lord. We know elsewhere (John 1:1–3, Col. 1:15–17) that, while Christ is subordinate to the Father (1 Cor. 11:3), He is personally responsible for the creation of the physical and spiritual worlds ("by whom are all things") and holds all things together by His own authority.

Dealing with the Consciences of the "Weak" (8:7–13): "However, not all men have this knowledge" (8:7)—indeed, not all *Christians* have this knowledge. A Christian who has come out of a pagan or idolatrous background may have difficulty in accepting the sovereignty of God the Father over his former beliefs in polytheism. By partaking of a meal that honors pagan gods, he may see nothing wrong with honoring them, *or* he may know full well that it *is* wrong (in his own mind) and yet does so anyway. The first scenario violates the doctrine of God; the second scenario violates his conscience. To "defile" one's conscience means to violate one's own understanding of what is right and wrong.[79] That which is permissible for one Christian's conscience may be sinful for another's. In any case, our standing before God is not determined (one way or another) by *food* (8:8) but sincere faith in God and obedience to His doctrine.

Christians have the liberty to eat meat but *not* to trample over a weak brother's conscience (8:9). One who invites a brother to participate in something that that person *knows* will violate his brother's conscience is not brotherly love but is sinful. (A "knowledgeable" Christian ought to *know better* than to do this!) Furthermore, even if one has no problem dining in a pagan establishment (such as an idol's temple) in pursuit of an excellent steak, weaker Christians who see him *may* be seriously offended by this (in regard to their conscience).[80] In fact, he may be giving endorsement to this other brother's former pagan lifestyle (8:10).[81] A "stumbling block" refers to anything that causes a hindrance to what needs to be done, or an occasion of tripping or falling (spiritually–speaking). "Weak" refers to a Christian who lacks spiritual knowledge, experience, or maturity—one who is still young in the faith. In this usage, "weak" *never* refers to one who chooses to be weak because of stubbornness, deliberate ignorance, disobedience, or laziness. Weakness, as used here, should be a phase and not a career.

Any injury deliberately inflicted against a weak brother, however, is also a slight against Christ Himself (8:11–12). Simply put: Christ's sacrificial death was *not* to protect my Christian liberty but to save souls; insisting on my Christian liberty at the *expense* of another's soul is to contradict His mission (Mark 10:45). As far as Paul is concerned, it is better for me to forego my Christian liberty than to be the cause for my brother's defiled conscience (8:13; see Rom. 14:15).

Questions

1.) "Knowledge makes arrogant, but love edifies" (8:1). But elsewhere, Paul *wants* Christians to "be filled with the knowledge of His [God's] will in all spiritual wisdom and understanding" (Col. 1:9). How are we to reconcile these two passages?

2.) Why is the practice of one's Christian liberties *at the expense of* a fellow Christian's conscience self–defeating and contradictory to the gospel?

3.) If it is (spiritually) reckless and irresponsible to dine in an idol's temple, then is it just as reckless and irresponsible to dine in a bar, nightclub, cocktail party, rave (etc.), even if we invoke our "Christian liberty" to do such things? Please explain.

4.) Whatever we do for or against a brother in Christ, we do for or against Christ (8:12; see also Mat. 25:31–46). How should this directly impact how we treat one another? Will God find favor with one who ignores this, even if he is a member of a "sound congregation"?

Lesson Twelve:

Paul's Use of Personal Liberty
(9:1–27)

Preachers and Compensation (9:1–14): In chapter 8, Paul taught that one must exercise his Christian liberty to with love and wisdom. He can also restrain or altogether deny his liberty in pursuit of a superior objective. Now (in chapter 9), Paul cites himself as an example of this teaching. While Paul's work as a preacher of the gospel deserves compensation, he foregos this liberty so that money will not interfere with the Corinthians' reception of his message.

Paul begins (9:1–14) by affirming that he himself possesses these rights as does any other Christian ("Am I not free?"—9:1), but he also has apostolic authority to determine how best to use them. In his role, he is not an equal with the Corinthians but serves as their instructor (recall 4:15). After all, *he* has "seen Jesus our Lord" (see Acts 9:3, 1 Cor. 15:8, etc.), they have not; they are *his* work in the Lord, not the other way around. "All free men were entitled to wages for work done. Only slaves worked without compensation. … [Paul was] more entitled to wages than an ordinary, less approved Christian teacher."[82]

Obviously, some of the Corinthians have challenged Paul's authority, possibly because he is not one of the original twelve apostles who initially preached in Jerusalem (9:3). No doubt this challenge comes from certain *Jews* in the Corinthian church (since Gentiles did not have a problem with this), who have succeeded in poisoning the minds of others against Paul. He meets this challenge directly and forcefully in the next epistle (*2 Corinthians*); for now, Paul exercises more discretion and restraint. He begins by affirming that he has Christian liberties regarding food just like all other Christians (9:4). He also has the *liberty* to marry a Christian woman, even though he has chosen *not* to do so (9:5).[83] Paul asks rhetorically: "Are Barnabas and I less faithful because we have declined support than those who *do* receive it?" (paraphrase of 9:6).[84]

Just as the soldier, vinedresser, shepherd, and farmer have the right to profit from their labors, so Paul has the right to profit from his (9:7). Such conclusions do not originate with men ("human judgment") but are in the Law of Moses (9:8–14; see Deut. 25:4). Just as an ox was allowed to eat as it worked the fields, and the priests had the right to receive their portion of the sacrifices which they prepared (Lev. 7:32–35, etc.), so Paul has the right to earn a living through his preaching of the gospel. The fact that he voluntarily declined that right (so the Corinthians would not accuse him of preaching for money), it remains his right all the same. And if Paul can lawfully make his living through the preaching of the gospel, then so can men do this today (9:14). Even Jesus said, "[T]he laborer is worthy of his wages" (Luke 10:7).

Paul's Choice to Forego Compensation (9:15–18): "But I have used none of these things" (9:15)—the "things" being the compensation for his work as a minister of the gospel. He is not saying this to try to change the situation; he is simply stating the facts. In fact, he would rather die than accept money from the Corinthians and invalidate his "boast"—a boast that is ironic, since there is nothing to boast about. When possible, he worked with his own hands to generate his own income (Acts 18:1–3). He also "robbed" other churches—a facetious statement—to avoid being a burden to the church in Corinth (2 Cor. 11:7–9). Yet, despite his best intentions, some Corinthians dismissed Paul's credentials *because* he did not ask money of them. Among the Greeks, to work for free or to perform menial tasks was a sign of inferiority.[85] In a sense, Paul faced a no–win situation: he was criticized whether or not he received compensation.

Yet, in Paul's mind, he pursued a higher objective than financial remuneration. Since Christ had made him an apostle, he felt compelled to serve Him regardless of how (or whether) he was compensated (9:16–18).[86] His "reward" was "to make full use of my right in the gospel"—in this case, the right to *decline* compensation—so that he would bring as many to Christ as possible.

"All Things to All Men" (9:19–27): However, Paul explains, he is not foregoing his liberties to please *them* but to serve Christ. This puts his actions in the proper light: he is "free from all men" (9:19) but *chooses* to be a "slave" to all men if it means an increase of Christ's heritage. He is willing to go to extreme lengths to accomplish this: he will assume the mindset—and culture, as much as was possible—of those whom he taught to win them to the Lord (9:20–22). Thus, Paul would "become" a Jew when teaching Jews, a Gentile when teaching Gentiles, etc., and "all things to all men." His objective is not to please himself but "so that I may by all means save some." To be a "fellow partaker [or, co–partner]"[87] of the gospel means that one may need to deny himself his "rights" (i.e., Christian liberties) for a much higher, nobler cause: to be a servant to those in need of a Savior (see Mat. 20:26–28, Mark 10:45).

Paul's statements here (in 9:20–22) need clarification: "To the Jews I became as a Jew"—obviously Paul is a Jew, so he is not *pretending* to be someone he is not. To "become a Jew" in the sense that is meant here is to put himself in the shoes of those who cling to Judaism—the practice of the Law of Moses *as well as* the rabbinic teachings that they regarded as being of equal authority as the Law (Mark 7:1–13, for example). In any case, he would adopt that man's mindset, his manner of reasoning, his method of justification, etc., to respectfully challenge his belief system with the gospel of Christ (as in Acts 9:20, 17:2–3, etc.).

Doing this did not make Paul *subject* to another person's belief system; he is not abandoning the gospel to *teach* it! But he is willing to set aside, for the sake of argument, his own knowledge to reach those who remain convinced of something inferior to his gospel.[88] His objective: "so that I may by all means save some" (9:22). "Some" means that *not all* will listen, despite his best efforts, but at least they will have opportunity to believe and obey. Paul is responsible only to preach the gospel, not for how people respond to it. By joining in the *work* of the gospel, he makes himself a fellow *partaker* of it (9:23).[89]

Such servitude, however, requires mental focus and self–discipline (9:24–25).[90] Paul draws on Grecian sports competitions to illustrate this. Running, boxing, horseracing, and chariot racing were common events at the well–known Isthmian Games (comparable to our modern Olympics) which were held near Corinth.[91] Paul did not just "run" but he ran *to win the prize*[92]; in seeking the salvation of "some" he never lost sight of his *own* salvation. No person should ever commit to becoming a Christian who does not have his own salvation as his goal *and* does everything in his power to obtain it (1 Peter 1:9).

Just because one enters the race, however, does not mean he will automatically or even easily finish it. Just as a runner will not win a race without exercise and training, so a Christian can still be "disqualified"[93] even though he may have been an effective evangelist. "Paul expresses a fear lest having laid down the gospel terms of salvation to others, he himself should be rejected for having failed to comply with the very rules which his own mouth had proclaimed (Luke 19:22, Rom. 2:1–3)."[94] "I run ... , I box ... , I discipline my body ... " (9:26–27)—such examples illustrate the *training, personal effort,* and constant *diligence* that are required to reach his objective. Paul disciplines his physical body to serve his spiritual obligations to the gospel, not the other way around.

Questions

1.) "If we sowed spiritual things in you, is it too much if we reap material things from you?" (9:11). Does this mean that "material things" are just as important as "spiritual things"? (Consider Rom. 15:27 in your answer.) On which of these two "things" do Christians often place higher *emphasis*, especially regarding compensating their preachers?

2.) For what exactly should a congregation compensate its minister(s)? How is this amount to be determined? Is this compensation a *gift* from the congregation or something he has a *right to receive*, as any other professional has in any other vocation?

3.) Are we (like Paul) to regard ourselves as "free from all men" (9:19)? If so, what exactly does this mean (in the context in which he said it)? What does it *not* mean?

4.) Are *all* Christians to "do all things for the sake of the gospel" (9:23)—or is this an obligation required only of full-time ministers? Please explain.

5.) Paul warned that it is possible for one to be "disqualified" even after having "preached to others" (9:27). What does he mean by this? What might contribute to one's disqualification? (Consider Luke 9:62, 14:26–27, 2 Peter 1:8–11, Rev. 2:4, and 3:2 in your answer.)

Lesson Thirteen:

Warnings Against Overconfidence (10:1–11:1)

Do Not Repeat Israel's Mistakes (10:1–12): Just as Paul was not immune to being "disqualified" of his reward despite being a preacher of the gospel (9:27), so the Corinthians are not immune to apostasy despite having been baptized into Christ. Paul underscores this fact with the historical example of Israel (10:1–4). Advantageously, they all:

❏ were "under the cloud"—i.e., the "pillar of cloud" that led them out of Egypt and through the wilderness (Exod. 13:21).

❏ "passed through the sea"—a reference to Israel's walk through the Red Sea (Exod. 14:13–22). The cloud and the sea served as symbols of *division* between those who belonged to God (Israel) and those who did not (Pharaoh and his army).[95]

❏ "were baptized into Moses"—i.e., in literally walking with Moses through the Red Sea. Figuratively, the ancient Hebrews were *immersed* in the teachings of Moses, and thus regarded themselves as his disciples (John 9:28, Acts 15:21).

❏ "ate the same spiritual food"—referring to manna, which was supernaturally provided and was thus "spiritual" in nature (Exod. 16:13–15, John 6:30–31).

❏ "drank the same spiritual drink"—this refers to the supernaturally–provided water from the rock which Moses struck (Exod. 17:6, Num. 20:8–11). "[A]nd the rock was Christ"—not literally, of course, but as a type or prefigure.

However, having all these advantages did not guarantee success to the Israelites. On the contrary, God was "not well–pleased" with their unbelief in His ability to perform (Heb. 3:7–4:11). Thus, they were "laid low in the wilderness" (10:5), an expression which carries a dual meaning: *humbled* by God's pronouncement of judgment; and *buried* in the wilderness wherein they had exhibited such unbelief.

Paul thus admonished the Corinthians not to become cocky or overconfident in their own knowledge, for they were not immune to Israel's mistakes (10:6). What happened to the Israelites was not an isolated, unique case, but serves "as examples for us"—i.e., Christians everywhere, for all time—and are meant as a warning. To avoid succumbing to their error:

❑ do not "crave evil things as they also craved" (10:6)—as when the Israelites longed for the food of Egypt and resented the manna which God had provided at no cost to them (Num. 11:4–6).
❑ "do not be idolaters ... " (10:7)—referring to the golden calf incident (Exod. 32:1–8).
❑ "nor let us act immorally ... " (10:8)—referring the Midianite women's seduction of Israelite men while Israel camped in the land of Moab (Num. 25:1–9), in which thousands of Israelites died because of the plague God sent upon them.
❑ "nor let us try the Lord" (10:9)—referring to Num. 21:4–9, when the people complained over the harsh conditions of the wilderness and were punished with "fiery serpents."
❑ "nor grumble ... " (10:10)—referring to Korah's rebellion against Moses and Aaron (Num. 16) for which God punished many Israelites by being buried alive, destroyed by fire, or killed by plague.[96]

"Now these things happened to them as an example" (10:11)—in other words, *since* they happened (and we have their record), we would do well to listen and learn (Rom. 15:4 and Heb. 4:11). In other words: just because one receives God–given privileges and advantages (as the Corinthians did), he still must *exercise obedient faith* in God (4:2). "Therefore let him who thinks he stands ... "—to "stand" with God in faith is salvation (Rom. 5:1–2, 11:20, and 14:4); to stand according to one's self–reliance or self–righteousness is (paradoxically) to *fall* from grace and be "severed from Christ" (Gal. 5:4).

"Flee from Idolatry" (10:13–22): "No temptation has overtaken you but such as is common to man ... " (10:13). "Temptation" [lit., trial; experience of evil solicitation; adversity (regarding one's faith)[97]] here has broad application. It is not only the enticement to commit a specific sin; it is also any occasion of human pride prevailing over human faith in God. Specifically, it has to do with the Corinthians who saw nothing wrong with

60

eating meat in an idol's temple. In any case, God does not allow a believer to be tempted beyond his limitations—*if* he seeks the will of God and does not knowingly put himself in an overwhelming situation. The emphasis here, however, is not on one's ability to withstand temptation but in God's merciful deliverance from it (the "way of escape"). It is not wrong to be tempted to sin; even Jesus was tempted personally by Satan (Mat. 4:1–11). One can "endure" temptation successfully by choosing to follow God *and at the same time* refusing to give life to any human desire that opposes Him (James 1:2–4, 13–16). Yet, one cannot "endure" *sin* without bringing upon himself a condemnation.

The lessons of Israel boil down to this: "flee from idolatry" (10:14). The Israelites paid dearly for their penchant for idolatry with severe losses, curses, and exile; many non–Jewish Corinthians, however, were unaware of these things. Paul's warning may also be summed up as follows: "Do not tamper with it [idolatry] by doubtful acts, such as eating idol meats on the plea of Christian liberty. The only safety is in *wholly shunning* whatever borders on idolatry."[98] Paul speaks from wisdom but challenges the Corinthians as to whether they will *listen* to it (10:15).

Carelessness with idolatry has no place in the Christian lifestyle or in Christian worship (10:16–17). When one shares in the cup and bread (blood and body, respectively) of the Lord's Supper, he *fellowships* with the One being honored in this (10:15–17). Likewise, when Israel shared in eating portions of the sacrifices (as in freewill offerings, another kind of "communion"), they joined in *fellowship* with the One on whose altar they offered these sacrifices (10:18).

The same is true when a Christian partakes of "the table of demons" (10:20)—i.e., eats a meal in an idol's temple that is knowingly dedicated to some idol or demon.[99] One cannot have communion with God *and* demons, since these have nothing in common (2 Cor. 6:14–16). While demons are real—Jesus did not cast out *pretend* demons—idols are the product of human imagination. Even though a Christian may know that an idol is nothing (10:19; recall 8:4), *by partaking of the meal* he may be viewed as an idolater (especially by a weak brother in Christ). Participating in idolatry is demonic in nature since it serves *the demons'* purpose and not God's. Thus, there must not be spiritual fellowship between unbelievers ("Gentiles") and Christians (10:20–21).[100] We cannot honor our Lord while dabbling in what belongs to Satan. This is true regarding the Lord's Supper and *any other activity* in which the Christian engages. "Or do we provoke the Lord to jealousy?" (10:22)—i.e., God will not share His holiness with man–made gods, and will punish those who insist upon doing this.

Just Because You *Can* Does Not Mean You *Should* (10:23–11:1): "All things are lawful … " (10:23; recall comments on 6:12): now Paul introduces the other side of the argument. Paul has been speaking about eating and drinking in an idol's temple. However, eating meat that has been sacrificed to an idol in a *different* context is not a moral crime. "Lawful" here involves those things we have the liberty to do that are not *prohibited* or specifically *regulated* by law (i.e., command or doctrine). But just because something is permissible does not mean it is always the best or acceptable course of action. "Profitable" means expedient, facilitative, contributing to that which is good, or that which improves the process by which something is done (as in 2 Tim. 3:16). "Edify" means to build up through (in this case) encouragement, exhortation, and/or positive examples.[101] Thus, in these few verses (10:23–24), Paul has established a template by which we can gauge *all* actions:

- ❑ If a given action is lawful AND profitable AND edifying, it is acceptable to God.
- ❑ If a given action is lawful but NOT profitable OR edifying, it is not acceptable to God.
- ❑ If a Christian liberty is knowingly NOT in (what God determines is) the BEST INTEREST of one's "neighbor," it should not be practiced.
- ❑ Every action must be done in GODLY LOVE (i.e., in the best interest, as God determines this, of *all* parties involved) and GODLY WISDOM (according to, and never in conflict with, God's doctrines) [implied].

Human expediency—that which *facilitates* the carrying out of apostolic doctrine—must never be confused or interchangeable with doctrine itself.[102] Doctrine comes from God; expediency is always a human decision based upon human judgment. While expediencies can be very wise in themselves, they are still inferior to divinely revealed doctrine.

While all foods are permissible to eat, it is never permissible in God's sight to offend another's conscience purposely or negligently (10:25–30). If meat is sold in the public market, then there is nothing wrong with it by itself. However, just because one's own conscience is "clear" (i.e., not offended) does not mean his actions will not offend the conscience of another. "Liberty is given to us, not in order to hurt ourselves and others, but in order to help ourselves and others." Thus, if a fellow Christian offers meat that he says *has* been sacrificed to an idol, Paul says to refuse it for the sake of that brother's conscience. We are not to be enslaved by the consciences of other men, but at the same time we are "to bear the weaknesses of those without strength and not just please ourselves" (Rom. 15:1). We are not to be judged for what is approved by God (10:30), but we must not flaunt our so–called Christian liberties at the expense of another's conscience. A balance is necessary, not just with food choices but with all choices.[103]

Whatever Christians do must be in honor of God (10:31; see Col. 3:17). While a basic teaching, this is always true and wise. "Give no offense … " (10:32)—not to *any person*: unbelieving Jews, non–Christian Gentiles, or Christians ("the church of God"). Paul offers himself as an example (recall 9:22): his objective was to *save* people—for this is *God's* objective—and not merely gratify his personal desires or protect his so–called liberties (10:33). His own liberties ("profit") must be surrendered in favor of seeking the spiritual well–being of others ("the many").

Thus, "Be imitators of me, just as I also am of Christ" (11:1): Paul is worthy of imitation only *when* and *because* he follows Christ. Thus, Paul is not the standard of excellent behavior, but Christ is. Furthermore, he is not asking the Corinthians to do anything that he himself does not practice. (This verse is more connected to chapter 10 than chapter 11. Chapter divisions were added many centuries later than when *1 Corinthians* was written.)

Questions

1.) Does "idolatry" always refer to the worship of man–made statues or images? If not, what kind of modern idolatry exists today? (Consider Eph. 5:3–6, Col. 3:5–7, and James 4:4 in your answer.)

2.) While God will not allow us to be tempted beyond what we are able to endure (10:13), it is also true that His providence is *conditional.*

    a.   What are these conditions?

    b.   Is it possible that God will providentially equip us to face what we *personally* or *at this moment* think we could never endure? Please explain.

3.) A Christian cannot partake of the "table of the Lord" *and* the "table of demons" because of the incompatibility between God and demons (10:21). Are there lifestyles that a Christian cannot partake of *today* that may be incompatible with his fellowship with Christ?

4.) What is wrong with following hypothetical examples? How can they be handled instead?

    a.   A newly baptized Christian believes it to be wrong to shop at a certain store that is owned by a denominational church; another Christian sees nothing wrong with shopping at this same store. One day, the second Christian asks his weaker brother to go shopping with him there.

    b.   One Christian listens to "Christian rock," while another finds it offensive to his conscience. While the two are riding together on a road trip, the first Christian (the owner of the car) plays an entire playlist of this music on his car stereo.

c. A Christian has long enjoyed smoking a pipe after dinner as a means of relaxation; his young teenage children, however, believe that smoking is a sin. One evening after dinner, this man lights up his pipe in the presence of his entire family and says to them, "If you don't like it, you can go outside."

d. Two Christians work at the same auto repair shop. One of these Christians believes it is permissible for him to take the shop's tools home with no intention of returning them; this practice violates the conscience of the other. One day, the first Christian says to the other (who needs a certain tool), "I tell you what: *I* will bring the tool from work to your house, so *you* can keep it with a clear conscience."

Lesson Fourteen:

Christian Women's Respect for Christian Men's Authority (11:2–16)

Preserving the Natural Order of Creation (11:2–10): This (11:2ff) begins not only a new topical subject but a new section to the entire epistle. Having dealt with several individual issues and concerns, Paul now turns his attention to the collective assembly of Christians (chapters 11–14). The Corinthians obviously had some problems with this, and possibly some questions concerning it. Specific subjects concerning the assembly of the saints are:

❑ The need for women to wear a head covering while prophesying and praying (11:2–16).
❑ Abuses of the Lord's Supper need to be corrected (11:17–34).
❑ The proper attitude toward the use of spiritual (miraculous) gifts (12:1–31).
❑ The need for Christian love for one another, regardless of spiritual gifts (13:1–13).
❑ The proper use of spiritual gifts, and the need for decency and order (14:1–40).

Paul begins this section with praise for the Corinthians for holding to the teachings that he had delivered to them while he was with them (11:2). Paul's praise may also be for their having asked for more direction or clarification rather than trying to form their own conclusions. (This is at a time when the written NT did not yet exist.)

This next topic—a Christian woman's head covering (11:3–16)—is often misunderstood and (thus) controversial.[104] Much of the difficulty stems from a failure to appreciate the *context* and *purpose* of this instruction. Also, contemporary Christians (who have been indoctrinated with feminism, humanism, and political correctness) often meet what Paul says about women's subjection to men with fierce resistance, defiance, and outright contempt. Such an approach, however, makes Scripture subordinate to modern thinking (or subjective opinions) rather than Christians listening to and obeying God's word. The fact remains, regardless of one's response to it: a woman's submission to men is a necessary part of her submission to God. These are not two separate subjects but the same.

The context of this passage specifically regards conducting the practices within "the churches of God" (11:16) with decency and order (1 Tim. 3:15, 1 Cor. 14:40). Paul begins with God's basic, overarching, and unchangeable position on the "place" of both men *and* women in the natural order of Creation: "Christ is the head of every man, and the man is the head of a woman, and God is the head of Christ" (11:3). Just as Christ submits Himself to His Father's authority—even though He (Christ) is "head" over *all* men but especially of His church (Col. 1:18)—so Christian women are to submit themselves to all Christian men generally (1 Tim. 2:12) but especially to their own husbands, *regardless* of whether these men are Christians (Eph. 5:22, 1 Peter 3:1).[105]

The appeal to "headship" (authority) is extremely important to God, and therefore must be important to us. Just as the Godhead has a "Father" (Eph. 4:6), all of Creation has a Creator, and the church has a divine "head" (Christ), so also the family requires proper leadership, as does every congregation (1 Tim. 3:4–5) and society in general. The husband's headship in marriage and his wife's submission to this headship parallels what already exists between the Father and the Son of God.

That having been said, Paul now provides the application (11:4–5). The specific regulation here concerns the covering of the (woman's) head, which is supposed to *differentiate* her distinctly from a man (see Deut. 22:5, in principle). In other words, just because a woman becomes a Christian does not give her the right to disregard her God–given "place" *as* a woman. The change in her spiritual status does not change or nullify her place in God's Creation or the natural *order* of Creation.

A mixed–gender assembly is a crucial factor in this entire discussion. The context of chapters 11–14 all have to do with mixed assemblies; there is not a single verse in any of these chapters that even hints at an *exclusively* male or female assembly. The assembly context has reference to *the church in Corinth*, not to male or female groups *within* the church in Corinth. Given this, the women's acts "praying or prophesying" must refer to things done in the presence of men; this necessarily includes (but is not limited to) the assembly of a congregation.[106]

"Praying" does not appear to be an ordinary prayer; Paul specifically instructed men to pray, not women (1 Tim. 2:8). However, he also did not forbid women to pray or prophesy (Acts 21:9, 1 Cor. 12:8–10). To prophesy is to speak while under the inspiration of the Spirit; "prophesying" necessarily identifies *both* actions are not ordinary or common functions. In the context of 1 Cor. 11:3–16 (and the larger context of 1 Cor. 11–14), the prayers and prophesying mentioned are the exercise of miraculous gifts of the Spirit (see 14:12–15). We should remember that the prophet Joel's prophecy (which Peter cited in Acts 2:16–21) stated that God's Spirit would be "poured forth" upon women as well as men.

Paul is not saying to women with such gifts, "Do not pray or prophesy." He only seeks to *regulate* these activities so that women did not violate an already–established *chain of authority*. If she leaves her head uncovered while representing the Holy Spirit (using His gifts), she shows rebellion, not submission. In this case, "she is one and the same as the woman whose head is shaved" (11:5–6): she has rebelled against God's placement of her in His natural order of Creation. By refusing to cover her head, she also refuses to accept the restraints which God has imposed upon her as a woman. In essence, she defied God's authority while simultaneously claiming to praise God through her gifts—a serious contradiction.

The head covering in question here must be something other than a woman's own hair, since this is a God–given characteristic of being a woman. In other words, whatever the "covering" was (and it is not important that we determine this absolutely), it must have been something that the woman *chose* to put over her head in order to deliberately distinguish herself from a man *while she engaged in the act of praying or prophesying* in the company of men.[107] This teaching only applies to women who fit the given scenario. Since God has not given us these gifts today, the instruction for a woman to necessarily cover her head is no longer relevant.

On the other hand, if a man prays or prophesies—again, these are miraculous works of the Spirit—with something on *his* head, then he also violates the natural order of Creation (11:4). He "disgraces his head" because he is identifying with *women* rather than with his God–given masculine identity (11:7). The context demands that this "covering" must refer to something other than a man's hair; it also demands that a man's head must *not* be covered when practicing the same things addressed for women—i.e., praying and prophesying in the Spirit. As "the image and glory of God" upon earth, he represents the highest *authority* on earth (recall 11:3), as evidenced by Adam's authority to name all the animals (Gen. 2:20) *as well as* Eve herself (Gen. 2:23, 3:20), and to subjugate all the earth (Gen. 1:28–30, 9:1–3). Thus, while man is "a little lower than the angels," God has put all things on earth in subjection to him (Heb 2:6–8). For this reason, a man "disgraces his head" (11:4) when he does what God expects only of a *woman* and does not respect God's authority given to *him*.

God has given the responsibility for headship to men; men did not choose this on their own; the church did not choose it for them. It is *God*, not mere genetics—and *never* one's personal choice—that makes a man *a man* or a woman *a woman*. Furthermore, it is God who placed woman in subjection to man for the following reasons (11:8–9):

❑   she was created *after* man (with relation to time or sequence).
❑   she was created *from* man (with relation to origin).
❑   she was created *for* man (with relation to purpose).

To ignore God's decision concerning gender and the responsibilities (or limitations) of it is to defy the natural order of Creation, which is to defy the Creator Himself. A woman's head covering shows submission to God's role as the Creator, and humbly accepts whatever conditions He has placed upon her. "Therefore the woman ought to have a symbol of authority on her head, because of the angels" (11:10)—this is a difficult passage, and some have admitted candidly that they do not completely understand it. In the most basic sense, it probably means that since the angels of God are ministers to the saints (Heb. 1:14) and are therefore in the presence *of* the saints in their worship, a woman needs to respect not only a man's God–given authority but also the presence of God's heavenly creatures. Their "authority," being greater than that of human beings (Heb. 2:7), deserves to be honored; the symbol of this honor is the veil/covering she wears upon her head.

A Mutual Understanding (11:11–16): "However, in the Lord … " (11:11)—meaning, as *all* Christians (men *and* women) are viewed with respect to Christ—"all things originate from God" (11:12). As children of God "in Christ," we are all "one" and the same (Gal. 3:28–29); no one is superior or inferior to another, regardless of gender.[108] But as *human beings*, a distinction must be made between men and women for the sake of authority and propriety, *not* domination or inferiority. Even so, in *both* cases—the spiritual context as well as the earthly—*both* sexes need each other and neither has independence from the other. And, while the first woman (Eve) came from a man (Adam), every person *since* then has been born of a *woman*—as ordained by God.

Having made that concession, Paul returns to a Christian woman who would dare to exalt herself among men while exercising gifts of the Holy Spirit (11:13–15). Paul has laid out his argument; now he calls upon the Corinthians to "judge" the matter for themselves (since they regard themselves as being so wise; recall 4:10). Just as "nature" distinguishes between men and women, those exercising spiritual gifts must also maintain this distinction. Whatever is of "nature" reflects the character of the Creator: He established the natural and original order of all things and expects us to honor this. "But if one is inclined to be contentious … " (11:16)—this is not Paul opening this issue for debate. Rather, he is saying in so many words, "This is the only valid position that we [apostles] have, and it is the same as what is taught in every church" (recall 4:17).

Two Distinctions:	
"Natural" context:	**When exercising spiritual gifts:**
❑ Head covering is provided "by nature" to all women in all contexts.	❑ Head covering is required of women who exercise spiritual gifts in the company of men.
❑ This covering is her (long) hair.	❑ This covering is unspecified but is something other than her hair.
❑ This has its origin in the Creation.	❑ This has its origin in the church during the time in which spiritual gifts were being exercised.
❑ This distinction recognizes the general, God–given authority that men have over women.	❑ This distinction recognizes this same authority, which is maintained even among those "in Christ."
❑ Head covering is provided "by nature" to men in all contexts (but it is no shame to him even if he loses his hair).	❑ Men are forbidden to wear an artificial head covering while exercising spiritual gifts since this violates God's placement of him in the natural order of Creation.

Questions

1.) With the great emphasis in our society concerning the "equality" of men and women, how might someone easily misrepresent or misunderstand this passage (11:2–16)?

    a. Is such misrepresentation/misunderstanding a problem only *outside* of the church today, or is it also a problem *within* the church? Please explain.

    b. Does God still require Christian women to be in subjection to Christian men? Does He still require Christian wives to be in subjection to their husbands?

2.) While we do not practice spiritual (miraculous) gifts today, what is the point of studying any passage that specifically deals with them? (There are several answers.)

3.) "For as the woman originates from the man, so also the man has his birth through the woman; and all things originate from God" (11:12). Why is this verse important and practical in understanding our relationship to each other (male to female) *and* to God (creation to Creator)?

Lesson Fifteen:

Correction of Abuses of the Lord's Supper (11:17–34)

The Corinthians' Abuse of the Lord's Supper (11:17–22): While he praised the Corinthians for having upheld doctrinal teachings that he had delivered to them (recall 11:2), Paul cannot praise them for their gross misconduct regarding the Lord's Supper (11:17, 22). What he hears from others concerning this misconduct distresses him; he does not *want* to believe it but has good reason to do so (11:18). Their abuses of this sacred ritual corrupt the purpose for their having assembled:

❑ Instead of edifying and strengthening one another, things are going in the opposite direction (11:17).

❑ Instead of "being of the same mind, maintaining the same love, united in spirit, intent on one purpose" (Phil. 2:2), they are creating self–serving divisions [lit., schisms] among themselves (11:18).

❑ Instead of humbly "[regarding] one another as more important than yourselves," and "not looking out for your own personal interests, but also for the interests of others" (Phil. 2:3–4), they segregate according to status, wealth, and human approval (11:19). Those who are "approved" are obvious since they are well–fed and made *drunk* in the process.

❑ Instead of coming together to "eat the Lord's Supper" in a sacred memorial, some are conducting this ritual as a social dinner in a festive or revelry–like atmosphere, while others are prevented from participating (eating) at all (11:20–21).

In doing all this, they have turned the Lord's Supper into a common meal, thus making no distinction between it and what one would do in his own house (11:22). (The church probably met in rich men's houses, which were the only ones big enough to accommodate large gatherings; this immediately put poorer brethren at a social disadvantage as well.) The Lord's Supper is not meant to be a meal for physical nourishment but to honor fellowship with Christ *and* fellow believers (recall 10:16–17), being filled with spiritual symbolism and soul-enriching implications.[109] To do otherwise *despises* or brings reproach upon the church of God—something Paul refuses to praise.

Taking the Lord's Supper in a Worthy Manner (11:23–34): With full apostolic authority, Paul thus reiterates the proper *context* and *solemnity* for observing the Lord's Supper (11:23–25; see Mat. 26:26–29). The fact that Paul "received" this from the Lord—we assume, in a vision or by divine revelation (see Gal. 1:11–12)—underscores the serious nature of this instruction. Jesus told us to "do this"—repeat this sacred rite—"in remembrance of Me." To *remember* Christ is not merely to call Him to mind or recall what He did. "Remember" in Scripture often means to *act* according to what has been promised, formerly taught, or established. To "remember" Christ in the Lord's Supper does *not* only mean, "Remember that He died for us"— this too!—but to obey Him *because* He died for us.

To properly and respectfully "remember" Christ, one must thoughtfully contemplate what the Lord's Supper symbolizes in the first place:

❑ The body *and* blood of Christ, acknowledging that He was a real, flesh-and-blood Person and not a myth or legend. Not only this, but the body and blood are mutually dependent: one is not possible without the other.
❑ Not only did He die for us, but we are to remember that He also *lived* for us: His death would have accomplished nothing if He had not offered His perfect, sinless, and virtuous *life* to God as an offering for sin.[110]
❑ Christ's sacrificial death was for *our* sakes—i.e., His body really *was* nailed to a cross for us, and His blood really *was* shed as an atonement for our sins.
❑ Christ fulfilled *all* sacrifices for sin in His "once for all" offering (Rom. 6:10, Heb. 10:10). Fifteen hundred years of animal sacrifices of the Law of Moses could not accomplish what Jesus' "once for all" death *did* accomplish (Eph. 3:11–12, Heb. 10:1–4).
❑ Christ endured unspeakable disrespect, humiliation, and torture to prove that He (the Son of God) was innocent of any injustice (Phil. 2:8, Heb. 12:2–3, and 1 Peter 2:21–24).
❑ Christ's fulfillment of the OT Scriptures through His sacrificial death (Luke 24:44–48).

- Ratification of a "new covenant" in which human sins are forgiven and "remembered no more" (Heb. 8:12, 9:15–26).
- Christ's resurrection (2 Tim. 2:8): we do not partake of the body and blood of a *dead man* but a risen, Living Savior—thus, we eat "living bread" and drink life–giving "blood" to sustain our souls (1 Peter 3:18).
- Christ's Second Coming (11:26): by remembering Christ's first advent (appearance), we also anticipate a second one (Acts 1:9–11).

Given the sacred nature of this communion, no one should partake of it in "an unworthy manner" without incurring divine condemnation ("judgment") (11:27). This refers to any irreverent, careless, or dishonorable attitude and/or behavior while conducting the holy ritual of "remembering" Christ. A "manner" speaks to procedure and propriety, not how one feels about himself.[111] The warning against an "unworthy manner" necessarily implies that there is a *worthy* manner.

"Examine" here (11:28–29) means "to (put to the) test; to prove by testing."[112] This testing must conform to *God's* criteria, not one's self–justification (recall 4:4; see 2 Cor. 10:18). One who fails to rightly observe the reason *for* the memorial—i.e., the body (person) and blood (life) of Christ—judges himself unworthy to partake of it.

Irreverence, because of deliberate ignorance *or* defiance, incites divine punishment. Just as the Corinthians received visible manifestations of the Spirit for their edification (1 Cor. 12:7–11), so God gave them visible manifestations of His punishment for their discipline (11:30). Whether these literal judgments—sickness and physical death[113]—still inflict Christians today cannot be known for certain but one can escape such judgment if he will observe the Lord's Supper properly in the first place (11:31). The design of God's temporary judgment is to save us from the ultimate judgment that the ungodly world will face in the future (11:32).

"So then … wait for one another" (11:33)—in other words, *observe the memorial together*, since it symbolizes unity and fellowship rather than division and segregation. Such "waiting" is in deference to one another: to eat the bread and drink the cup *together* indicates that no Christian is superior or inferior to another.[114] "But if anyone is hungry, let him eat at home" (11:34)—i.e., the *assembly* is not the time or place to partake of physical nourishment. The reason for the assembly is to partake of this *sacred* meal which commemorates the Savior's life and great sacrifice. No other meal is to equal or be confused with this one.

Questions

1.) Separations ("divisions" and "factions") are obvious signs of a congregation in trouble. In the Corinthian church (11:18–19), what was causing these separations? (There are several possible answers.)

2.) What are two reasons given in 11:23–26 that partaking of the Lord's Supper is (or can be regarded as) an act of faith?

3.) Self–examination for partaking of the Lord's Supper indicates some form of mental and spiritual preparation (11:28). What exactly does this "examining" involve? Is there any other preparation required of us?

4.) Do Paul's statements in 11:22 ("Do you not have houses in which to eat and drink?") and 11:34 ("If anyone is hungry, let him eat at home") condemn eating and drinking in a church–owned building? Or do these have to do with separating the Lord's Supper from any common meal (i.e., emphasis on the *observance* vs. what happens in a *building*)?

Lesson Sixteen:

The Unity of the Body of Christ (12:1–31)

The Gifts of the Spirit (12:1–11): "Now concerning" (12:1) indicates Paul's further address of questions the Corinthians had presented to him (recall 7:1 and 8:1). "Gifts" (in 12:1) clearly involves miraculous "manifestation[s] of the Spirit" (see 12:7).[115] The purpose of these gifts was to confirm God's truth in lieu of a written record of the gospel. Once this record was completed (Jude 1:3), such gifts or proofs were no longer needed.

Man–made, mute, and lifeless idols cannot impart gifts of miraculous speech, power, and healings (12:2). Unconverted "pagans" [lit., Gentiles] worship idols, which derive their utterance and power entirely from human effort. God's Holy Spirit, however, is a divine member of the Godhead with His own identity and function.[116] By imparting miraculous gifts He proves the supreme power and authority of Christ who has *sent* the Spirit for this purpose (John 16:13–14, Acts 1:8, and 2:33). Thus, the Spirit cannot be identified with anyone who would oppose Christ, and no one can assert Christ's divinity apart from the Spirit's endorsement (i.e., through miraculous prophecy) (12:3). These gifts serve as a witness or testimony to the gospel truth that was preached first by Christ, then His apostles (Heb. 2:3–4).

As one Spirit distributes and oversees all spiritual gifts (12:4), the purpose of His gifts are to unite and edify God's people, not cause jealousy and division. "Varieties of ministries" and "varieties of effects" do not require varieties of "gods"—like what the Corinthians were accustomed to believing according to their pagan ways (12:5–6; see Gal 4:8–9). The gifts are not given to exalt the one exercising them but are "for the common good"—for the benefit of the entire body (congregation).[117] While there are nine different gifts (or classification of gifts) mentioned here, they are all *given* and *governed* by the "same Spirit" (12:8–11). From this (and related passages), we conclude that this "one Spirit" determines:

- the purpose of the gifts which He bestows.
- how the gifts are bestowed—i.e., through the laying on of the apostles' hands (Acts 8:14–17, 19:6, and 2 Tim. 1:6).
- who receives a gift (or effect)—and who does not (12:29).
- who receives what *kind* of gift (i.e., the distribution of gifts—12:11, 18).
- the proper context in which gifts are to be used—for the "common good" (12:7).
- the limitations of those gifts—i.e., they cannot be used for selfish reasons (2 Tim. 4:20) or in any way that would "test" God (Mat. 4:7).
- the duration of those gifts (i.e., they are given only while the purpose for them remains; once the purpose is fulfilled, such gifts will no longer be necessary [implied]).

These gifts were not for show or entertainment. Rather, they confirmed God's revealed word in the absence of the written NT that we enjoy today. The gifts mentioned here are as follows (12:8–10):

- "the word of wisdom"—likely this means wisdom granted by necessity.
- "the word of knowledge"—likely, this refers to the giving and verification of knowledge being introduced into or taught within the Corinthian church.
- "faith"—not *personal* faith, because that is something every believer must give to God (and never something God gives to *him* or *her*). Here, the gift must be a strengthening, emboldening, or reassurance of *personal* faith during difficult trials.[118]
- "gifts of healing [or, healings]"—a self–evident gift.
- "effecting of miracles [or, works of power]"—a general category involving all non–specific demonstrations of miraculous power.
- "prophecy"—not merely foretelling the future (although this, too; see Acts 11:27–28), but also the speaking and confirmation of divine truth.
- "distinguishing [or, discerning] of spirits"—a miraculous discernment of those who preach, as to whether they are of God or influenced by demons (1 Tim. 4:1, 1 John 4:1).
- "{various} kinds of tongues"—lit., the utterance of a genuine language which is not previously known to the one speaking it (Acts 2:3ff, 10:46, 19:6, etc.). "Tongues" is from the Greek *glossa* [lit., tongue; language]; tongue–speaking is called *glossolalia*.[119] "It was not mere gibberish or

jargon like the modern 'tongues,' but in a real language that could be understood by one familiar with that tongue as was seen on the great Day of Pentecost when people who spoke different languages were present."[120]

❏ "interpretation of tongues"—the ability to understand what was being said by the one speaking in tongues.

Regardless of the variety or nature of the gifts, *one Spirit* produces and oversees all of them, according to what He determines is best suited for the person, occasion, and need (12:11).

The Unity of the Spirit in the Church (12:12–26): While Paul's use of "one body" here (12:12) specifically concerns the Corinthian church, it does no harm to the passage to extend it to the entire body of Christ (i.e., the worldwide, spiritual church; the entire brotherhood). Just as the human body has "many members [or, organs]," the body of Christ has many members (a living organism)—but it is still *one body*. Christ's church—His body (Col. 1:18)—is also *one*: it is singular, united, and indivisible (recall 1:13).

Regardless of gender, ethnicity, or social status, "we were all baptized into one body" (12:13; see Acts 2:41, 47). The fact that this baptism was "by [or, in] one Spirit" does not make it a so–called "spiritual baptism," or an alleged "baptism of the Holy Spirit," as modern charismatics commonly assume. Paul speaks of an *individual experience*, whereas the Spirit's baptism of Christ's church is a *collective one* (i.e., of all Jews first, then of all Gentiles; see Acts 2:14–18).[121] "There is no reason to think that 'we were baptized' refers to anything other than baptism in water (together with all that this outward rite signified)."[122]

The most natural meaning of Paul's use of "by one Spirit" means according to His authority, instruction, and oversight.[123] Our common baptism, and the Spirit's sanctification that we all receive upon that baptism (1 Peter 1:2), make us one spiritual body (i.e., Christ's church). God's people are identified by one singular Spirit, not many spirits (or attitudes, personalities, or teachings). We "are all one in Christ Jesus" (Gal. 3:28), not many different kinds or brands of Christians. Our baptism *into* Christ is what creates this new, united relationship (Gal. 3:26–27).

The next passage (12:14–26) deals with one overarching subject: the *equalizing* of all members of the body of Christ. Again, "body" here means the *entire* community of believers everywhere but can refer *in principle* to a single congregation. Paul uses the term in a dual sense throughout this chapter.

Just as a standalone part of the human body cannot function apart from the context of the entire body, so a Christian cannot function *in the way God intended* apart from the rest of the body of Christ. Just as a hot ember needs the rest of the fire to keep it hot—and the fire itself is comprised of many embers—so Christians individually share in something bigger than any one of them. Since we are all brought together in the same body by the same Spirit, we are expected to *work together in cooperation* with "the same mind, maintaining the same love, united in spirit, intent on one purpose" (Phil. 2:2).

Miraculous gifts of the Spirit did not interfere with this cooperation but *facilitated* it. The fact that some gifts might be more esteemed than others, some members might have more responsibility than others, or one member's work may be more visible or influential than another's, is irrelevant to these points (12:14–17). No member is useless or expendable to Christ—and thus (ideally) not to any of us. It is God who has "placed" us wherever He wants and imparts to us whatever gifts or talents he wants us to exercise for His glory (12:18–21).

Paul presents us with a paradox: those with "honor" (i.e., who are esteemed, comely, or presentable) are to bring honor to "our less presentable members" (12:22–24a). This is only accomplished when each member (the so-called honorable as well as those who appear to lack this same honor) maintains a proper attitude: each one contributes to the others' needs, thus each one is made equal in Christ.

The intended effect of such equal distribution of "honor" throughout the body is that there be *no divisions* based upon appearance, status, gifts, talents, responsibilities, etc. (12:24b–25). "In Christ" is a leveling ground in which all believers stand on equal footing and where all such human, social, or earthly distinctions are unnecessary (Gal. 3:28–29). Thus, even if one member suffers or is honored, so all share in that suffering or rejoice in that honor (12:26; see Rom. 12:10). Christian fellowship, whether in an individual congregation or the entire brotherhood, is not a competition, rivalry, or pursuit of personal glory at the expense of someone else.

Various Gifts and Appointments, but One Body (12:27–31): As spiritual gifts vary, so do their functions (or, appointments) within the church (12:27–30). We *all* "are Christ's body, and individually members of it" (12:27) but we do not all have the same role, function, or responsibility. From heaven's vantage point, we are all equals; however, the church on earth is comprised of different levels of talents and works. There is nothing wrong with recognizing various distinctions, capabilities, and statuses among Christians; this is natural, expected, and even necessary. For example, we cannot have leaders in the church if we do not acknowledge some men *as* leaders, and that they have leadership abilities that other men do not possess. And, we cannot have husbands leading the marriage relationship without their wives honoring this.

Even so, these different functions and responsibilities all contribute to the success of the one body. Just as the human body is not one big eyeball, or one giant ear, so not *all* members will be apostles, or prophets, or teachers, etc. Just as the Spirit determines the spiritual gifts, so He determines the functions within the body; all things work toward the "common good" (recall 12:7; see Rom. 8:28 and Eph. 4:11–13). It is not our place to question the appointments that God has made; it is ours to accept whatever He has given each one of us to do.

There is nothing wrong with desiring "the greater gifts," as men might categorize them (12:31). The Spirit distributes these gifts according to His own wisdom and authority, but someone may seek a different gift through prayer, petition, and humility (Mat. 7:7–8); otherwise, Paul's encouragement to "desire the greater gifts" has no meaning. Whether the Spirit grants such a request is up to Him. Regardless, Paul says that there is *one* "excellent way" in which *all* members can participate. "The sense is, 'Seek the better gifts, and moreover I show you an excellent way to do it.'"[124] This is a segue way into the next chapter.

Questions

1.) Since the Spirit no longer imparts to Christians the ability to perform miracles, are we to conclude then that the Spirit is no longer active within the church?

    a.   If He is not, how are we to be "led by the Spirit" (Rom. 8:14) and produce "fruit of the Spirit" (Gal. 5:22–23)? Can mere words in the Bible fulfill God's promises for divine action in the lives of believers?

    b.   If He *is* still active, in what ways *does* He work in the lives of believers today? (And are we limited in knowing all that He does for us?)

2.) The Spirit's gifts worked to the "common good" of God's people (12:7). Does an appeal to the "common good" serve as an ideal principle today for shepherds, preachers, heads of household, and all members of a given congregation? Please explain.

3.) Because we are all part of the same body (of Christ), does this mean we all have equal say and equal responsibilities as Christians?

    a.   If we do, how can anyone exercise leadership (if we are all "leaders")?

    b.   If we do not, how are we to determine when one person's decision or responsibility is to be used rather than another's?

4.) Does 12:14–26 necessarily imply that participation in the "body" requires a literal assembling together with fellow Christians? Are we able to carry out our responsibilities of cooperation and mutual edification by choosing *not* to assemble with the church?

Lesson Seventeen:

The Greatest Gift of All
(13:1–13)

This chapter contains some of the most eloquent and powerful expressions of love ever written. While Paul is not intending to provide a comprehensive theological perspective on "love," nonetheless what he *does* say is remarkable—and profound in its brevity. Indeed, love is the most excellent "way" to demonstrate God's power to the world—even better than through the exercise of miraculous gifts.

The message is clear: one who has a miraculous gift but *does not have love* is "nothing"—that is, he is of no profit to himself or the body of Christ (13:1–3). Or if one's attitude is unmoved by godly love, it does not matter what else he is or does—in the end, he loses everything. Paul uses some of the more highly valued gifts to make his point: speaking in tongues[125] without love is just noise; prophecy, knowledge of God, and (claims of) great personal faith without love are pointless; etc. Even great displays of sacrifice—including one's own martyrdom—without love "profits me nothing." The Corinthians thought highly of men with eloquence (such as Apollos; see Acts 18:24) who are masters of language and oration; to speak with the exalted language of an *angel* is even more admired. Yet, Paul says that all such demonstrations of ability *without love* are exercises in futility.

"Love" here [Greek, *agape*] means to selflessly act in another's best interest. Just because someone claims to "love," or to have love, does not mean he (or she) conforms to Paul wrote. Emotions, passion, infatuation, sexual attraction, and romantic intimacy often pass for "love" today but have nothing to do with what Paul describes. Human love, left uninspired or unconditioned by divine influence, always falls short of and is inferior to God. We can imitate God's love but cannot duplicate it; God did not learn how to love by watching us (or, by His experience with us, as a mother learns to love her child) but we learn how to love supremely by watching Him. God's love is the source of all Christian love, never the other way around; all love that contradicts God's love also contradicts His own holy nature since "God is love" (1 John 4:8). Love is not a mere nicety or pious virtue; it is the *foundational premise* upon which all other moral laws and principles rest (Rom. 13:8–10, Gal. 5:13–14). Love is the "royal law" of the kingdom of God (James 2:8), the King Himself having demonstrated it to us in full (1 John 4:9–10).

Godly Love Defined (13:4–7): God is the One who defines "love" in this chapter—and in the context of the Christ's gospel; modern, emotional, or personal standards cannot redefine it for us. Your love may be grand in comparison to mine, yet Paul is not talking about *your* or *my* love but God's. Just because two people love each other does not mean they imitate God's love. Human love is always self-serving, in one respect or another; we are only at our finest hour when we do our best to imitate God's love. Christ is the greatest expression of God's love we have ever seen; to love one another as He has loved us (John 13:34–35) is to love like what Paul is about to describe. Thus, godly love is (13:4–7):

- ❏ **"patient"** or long–suffering—it bears, endures, and even suffers, but only for the noblest of causes. Patience is the manifestation of forbearance (despite adversity) and/or restraint (despite deserved punishment) in anticipation of a particular (godly) objective (2 Peter 3:9).
- ❏ **"kind"**—benevolent, gentle, tender, affectionate; not sour, harsh, or mean.
- ❏ **"not jealous"**—not envious of (or coveting) another's happiness, blessing, or prosperity.
- ❏ **"does not brag"**—does not boast or vaunt its own accomplishments.
- ❏ **"is not arrogant"**—not inflated (or, puffed up) with pride or vanity. Bragging describes what someone *does*, whereas "arrogant" describes what someone *is*.
- ❏ **"does not act unbecomingly"**—is not indecent or unseemly; behaves itself; acts properly, discreetly, and gracefully.
- ❏ **"does not seek its own"**—i.e., is unselfish; does not pursue happiness at another's expense; seeks another's best interests ahead of one's own (Phil. 2:3–5).

- ❑ **"is not provoked"**—is not agitated, does not rush to anger; is not sudden, rash, or impetuous; is not instigated or baited by someone's taunting or the persuasion of evil.
- ❑ **"does not ... suffered"**—is not malicious or prone to evil; does not seek harm, vengeance, or retaliation, despite whatever harm is done to *it* (Rom. 12:17–20, 13:8–10). Barclay translates this: "does not store up the memory of any wrong it has received."[126]
- ❑ **"bears all things, believes all things, hopes all things, endures all things":** love is the finest, most noble virtue, period. Love always seeks to forgive and restore, freely offers the benefit of doubt, is optimistic, and does not try to hurry one's reception to it. It is pure, timeless, and transcendent; it imposes itself upon no one, and yet cannot be destroyed by anyone (Rom. 8:35–39). Take love out of the picture, and there is no more reason for life, mercy, grace, or justice; there is no more *reason*.

Love's Supremacy and Endurance (13:8–13): "Love never fails" (13:8)— even though everything else in this life most certainly *will* fail because human vice and greed have corrupted it. God will destroy the entire world, but those who love Him—and who love as He loves—will "abide forever" (1 John 2:15–17). "We know in part and we prophesy in part" (13:9)— despite the special knowledge and prophetic abilities with which the Corinthians have been blessed, there is still much that they do not know. Not only this, but the spiritual gifts to which they have given so much emphasis will disappear: these gifts were never meant to last forever or complete the believer. If the Corinthians all exercised godly love, then their divisions, infighting, and jealousies would vanish. What brings anyone to completion is *godly love*: anyone can have this gift and everyone will benefit from it.

The "perfect" here (13:10) is often thought to be the completion of the gospel; this is based on passages like James 1:25 and Jude 1:3. It is perhaps more accurate to see this as a comparison rather than an explanation: when the "perfect" comes, whatever is less–than–perfect will be superseded.

The temporary (required to fulfill the objective):	The permanent objective (fulfillment of the need):
Childhood	Manhood
Engagement (betrothal)	Marriage
Apprenticeship	Journeyman
Spiritual (miraculous) gifts to establish Christ's church and reveal His gospel to mankind	An established church *and* a fully–revealed gospel
An earthly body	A spiritual body (1 Cor. 15:42–49, 2 Cor. 5:1)
First heavens and earth (physical dwelling place)	New heavens and new earth (or, spiritual dwelling place; 2 Peter 3:11–13, Rev. 21:1–4)

Paul's analogy of a boy becoming a man explains the temporary nature of miraculous gifts in comparison to the overall growth of Christ's body (13:11). The church, in Paul's day, is still a "boy"; once the gospel is fully revealed, the gospel is preached throughout the world (Col. 1:23), and the church reaches maturity (Eph. 4:11–16, where the "child" imagery is used again), then the gifts will be done away with.

To further illustrate, consider the construction of a large building. As the building phase moves toward completion, all temporary phases are ended. Scaffolding, for example, is necessary to build this structure but only until the building is finished. Once the construction is complete, the scaffolding is no longer necessary and is removed. Buildings are not built to use scaffolding; rather, scaffolding is used to build buildings. This is analogous to spiritual gifts: the gospel message is not revealed to confirm the gifts, but the gifts are given to confirm the gospel message. Once the message has been revealed and recorded for all time, gifts are no longer necessary. Gifts of prophecy, tongues, and (miraculous) knowledge are "partial" because they are temporary and transitional, but the "perfect" is permanent and transcendent.

On a more practical level, there are two reasons why we do not see God imparting miraculous gifts to Christians today.

- ❏ **First**, there is no need for them. If God's record of His miracles cannot stand on its own merit, then offering repeated miracles to say the same thing and come to the same conclusions will not do any better.[127] The verdict is in; God's truth has been once for all revealed, established, and recorded; there is no other legitimate verdict to reach.

- ❏ **Second**, there is no one to impart these miracles. Except for the initial representatives for the Jews (the twelve apostles—Acts 2:1–11) and the Gentiles (Cornelius and company—Acts 10:44–48), the Holy Spirit only gave His gifts through the laying on of the apostles' hands (Acts 6:6–8, 8:14–17, 19:6, etc.). As the apostles died out, so did the ability to transmit this power in the manner prescribed by the Spirit.

"For now we see in a mirror dimly" but this will not always be the case (13:12).[128] Paul's statement here takes us far beyond the discussion of spiritual gifts but speaks of our human limitations in earthly life. For now, we are limited in what we know, but someday—in the life to come—we will know "fully" whatever there is to know. For now, we exercise human faith; in the hereafter, there will be no need for this, since we will see God face to face (13:13). For now, we exercise hope in what we have not yet seen or received; in the hereafter, there will be no need for this, since what we have hoped for will be ours (see Rom. 8:24–25). But *love* is greater than faith and hope, since godly love will never end, and will continue in the hereafter just as it has always been.

Questions

1.) In 13:1–3, Paul referred to three different realms in his illustration: what he *does*, what he *possesses*, and what he *gives*. None of these is meaningful if he does not have love. On a more practical level, what use is it if a Christian does not have love even though he:

    a.   is a faithful churchgoer, never missing a service or meeting?
    b.   greets people with a smile and a handshake?
    c.   sings spiritual hymns more beautifully and proficiently than all others?
    d.   gives more money to the church than all others?
    e.   prays eloquent, thought–provoking prayers?
    f.   is well–versed in the Scriptures and can teach a Bible class?
    g.   serves as a deacon or elder?
    h.   is a gifted preacher who offers fine, stirring lessons?
    i.   is a good provider (husband) or a submissive spouse (wife)?
    j.   is a hardworking and attentive parent?

2.) Whatever Paul said about "love" (in 13:4–7) was about *God* since "God is love" (1 John 4:8). To imitate God's love (Eph. 5:1), must we adopt these same qualities in our own love? Or is it sufficient that we simply "love" in whatever way seems right in our own eyes? Please explain.

3.) Paul wrote, "When I became a man, I did away with childish things" (13:11). What "childish things" does every Christian need to "do away with" to become a mature believer? (There are several answers.)

4.) What makes love "the greatest" over faith and hope? Is there *any* virtue greater than love (see Col. 3:12–14)? If love *is* so "great," should we spend *less* time developing this virtue or *more* time on it than anything else?

Lesson Eighteen:

The Proper Use of Spiritual Gifts in the Assembly (14:1–40)

The Purpose for the Gift of "Tongues" (14:1–19): Having discussed the *greatest* gift (love), Paul now returns to the subject of *spiritual* gifts (14:1). It is important to remember that his instruction has to do with what happens *in the assembly* without addressing other contexts. While everyone can pursue love, God does not impart everyone with miraculous ability. Paul, for his part, puts prophecy as the most profitable of all gifts, and then offers his explanation (14:2–3). One who speaks in a foreign tongue does not know what he is saying (until another interprets it); he speaks to God but not everyone immediately benefits. Prophecy, on the other hand, benefits everyone immediately. "Our modern *preaching* is the successor of *prophecy*, but without the inspiration."[129]

Prophecy—again, not merely foretelling the future but revealing God's truth—provides "edification and exhortation and consolation" (14:3–5). These are dominant themes in this chapter and are major objectives even today in the preaching of the gospel.

- ❑ "Edification" is the process of building up (something)—in this case, of believers, and the church in general. Edification of the church is far more important than whatever personal edification one derives from speaking in tongues. Worship must never descend into a self–serving experience.
- ❑ "Exhortation" [Greek, *paraklesis*] is translated elsewhere as comfort, consolation, encouragement, and (positive) urging.[130]
- ❑ "Consolation" is very close to exhortation but has more to do with offering comfort in place of doubt, fear, or anxiety, whereas exhortation (here) has to do with a general encouragement to do well and stay the course.

Paul reiterates his point concerning the greater benefit of prophesying over tongue–speaking (14:6). What good, he says rhetorically, would it be to hear tongues without knowing what is being said? Prophecy, however, involves "revelation," "knowledge [of God]," and "teaching," from which all can benefit. The overall lesson here is that the improper use of spiritual gifts will not be edifying, defeating their entire purpose. Even musical instruments must be used properly to produce an understandable melody; and a "bugle [or, trumpet]" must be played in such a way that men can prepare for battle (14:7–8). Likewise, if one speaks in foreign tongues but no one knows what is being said, then nothing is gained (14:9). All languages (or, voices) in the world are intelligible to *some* but not to *everyone*. If one speaks a language that is unknown to himself and his listening audience, he sounds no different than a foreigner ("barbarian") does to us today (14:10–11).

Once again, "edification of the church" (14:12) is the goal, not merely speaking in tongues. It is clear in this chapter that the tongue–speaking Paul describes is not a spasmodic, uncontrollable experience that is *supposed to be* controlled. Confusion and disorder must never characterize the delivery of God's message, the conduct of His people, or the atmosphere of our assemblies. God's people are to present their worship of God as intelligible and organized.

Praying in tongues (as an exercise of a miraculous gift) does not help the listening assembly or even the one offering the prayer (14:13–15). An "ungifted" person—i.e., one who does not have spiritual gifts—will not be able to comprehend, endorse, or even "amen" that which he cannot know (14:16). Tongues are a sign (or, testimony) to unbelievers but only if used properly; otherwise, they produce the exact opposite effect (i.e., madness and confusion). Tongues are *not* to show off an ability one possesses but are for the benefit of the entire group (14:17–19). Better to say a few edifying words, Paul says, than many words that no one can understand.

"Let All Things Be Done for Edification" (14:20–40): "Brethren, do not be children in your thinking … " (14:20)—a mild rebuke to the Corinthians' immaturity concerning spiritual gifts. Paul cites the Law to show that tongues fail to accomplish anything if no one understands them (14:21).[131] Furthermore, tongues are meant to convince unbelievers (non–Christians) more so than believers; prophecy, on the other hand, is meant to edify believers more so than unbelievers (14:22–24). Paul gives the realistic example of an unbeliever walking into an assembly where many are speaking in tongues, but no one is interpreting. To that person, it sounds like *gibberish*, and he will conclude that the Christians there are "mad," meaning *out of their mind.*

Paul now turns his attention to the proper use of spiritual gifts in the assembly (14:26–40). **First,** "let all things be done for edification" (14:26; recall 10:23). **Second,** let everything that is done "when you assemble" (14:26) be done properly and orderly so as not to bring reproach upon the church. God expects His people to conduct themselves in a dignified, respectful, and reverent manner—even (and especially) when exercising spiritual gifts. The fact that God no longer gives these gifts to the church today does not nullify the appropriate *conduct* expected of Christian assemblies.

Paul then gives specific instructions to those who speak in tongues. They must be limited to two or three speakers in each assembly; if no interpreter is present, then they are to "keep silent in the church" (14:27–28).[132] Those who speak in tongues are to speak in turn—not over the top of each other— to prevent chaos and confusion (14:29). Similarly, only two or three are to prophesy, while the others are to "pass judgment" (i.e., make discernment) as to whether the thing spoken is genuinely from the Holy Spirit (1 John 4:1). Also, if one receives a revelation (from God), then the other must "keep silent" (14:30). In other words, people are to speak in turn ("one by one") to demonstrate decency and order.

"[T]he spirits of prophets are subject to prophets" (14:32) means that a person with a miraculous gift *also* has full control over the time and place in which he exercises it. (The "spirit" here can only refer to the spirits of *men*; God's Spirit is never subject to "prophets.") The idea of the Holy Spirit overtaking a person and forcing him to move, speak, or perform a miracle against his free will is foreign to the NT record. Confusion is not something that comes from God but only from *people* (14:33a).[133]

True worship of God produces peace, dignity, and seriousness. This does not mean we cannot be *human* in an assembly; it means we are not to allow human emotions, God–given talents, or personal preferences to rob the assembly of its purpose: to worship God *and* edify one another. No one—

regardless of his "gift"—has the right to create confusion and disorder within the church. Paul is not giving a different instruction to the Corinthians than what he has taught everywhere (14:33b; recall 4:17 and 11:16).[134]

The present context must determine whatever conclusions we draw from Paul's instruction for women to "keep silent" (14:34–35). "Women" is from the Greek word *gune*, which can mean brides, women, or wives, depending on the context.[135] The fact that these "women" have husbands (14:35) means *wives* are meant here. Women are to "subject themselves" to all men (recall 11:3) but to their *husbands* specifically (Eph. 5:22). Obviously, Paul is addressing a problem he has encountered elsewhere—namely, that of wives interrupting the service to ask questions of their husbands, possibly concerning their (husbands') own exercises of gifts. Paul says, in effect, that this is disruptive, unnecessary, and needs to stop.

Paul is not saying that women can *never* make *any vocal sound* in *any* assembly.[136] This takes Paul's words out of context. Traditionally, people have interpreted this passage to mean that women cannot say *anything* in an assembly. Often, this conclusion overlooks or ignores the passage's specific purpose in the first place. Paul cites "the Law" (here, referring to the Law of Moses) to make his point—a crucial piece of information. The Law says nothing about women not speaking in an assembly; however, it *does* say that wives are to be in subjection to their husbands ("he will rule over you"— Gen. 3:16). The issue here has far more to do with wives' submission to their own husbands than it does to whether a woman can utter a word in an assembly.

In 14:34–35, "silent" is a *voluntary* action expected of the woman (wife), not something imposed upon her by others. It is not the church's responsibility to silence Christian women; it is every Christian woman's responsibility to recognize and subject herself to the God–given expectations of a woman *and* a wife. Paul does not say, "Church, silence your women!" Rather, he puts the responsibility upon the *wives* to silence *themselves* in whatever context would prove to be disruptive (and thus not edifying) to the assembly ("[they] are to subject *themselves*"—14:34, emphasis added). This "silence" is not meant to suppress a woman's worship of *God* but to keep her from disregarding or violating her *husband's* authority over her which God had given him (Eph. 5:22, 33).

Paul then reminds the Corinthians that he has greater authority (as Christ's apostle) than they do, and that he does not learn from them, but they are to receive *his* instruction (14:36). One who claims to be God's prophet or even spiritual–minded will respect Paul's authority (14:37). His teaching—particularly, in this letter—is not his own but is "the Lord's commandment." (The only exceptions to this are where Paul says otherwise, as in 7:6, 12, 26, and 40.) One who refuses to submit to an apostle's authority renders himself unfit for providing instruction to others; in fact, "he is not [to be] recognized" by the church" (14:38, bracketed words added). On the other hand, those who belong to God will listen to His words (John 8:47).

Paul sums up what he started in 14:1: "desire earnestly" the gift of prophesy but not at the expense of tongue–speaking (14:39). Regardless, "all things must be done properly and in an orderly manner" (14:40)—specifically, in the assemblies of the saints (recall 14:33). This principle, of course, extends to Christians in any context: marriage (Eph. 5:22–27), home (1 Tim. 3:4–5), in public (Phil. 2:14–15), and in the company of unbelievers (Col. 4:5). "Properly" implies becomingly, appropriately, and respectfully—the *way* Christ wants things done; "in order" implies structure, stability, and organization—the *practice* itself.

Questions

1.) Two major themes of this chapter are *edification* and *orderliness*. Are these principles still required in *all* assemblies of Christians today, or are they limited to spiritual gifts?

2.) The exercise of spiritual gifts was a mature situation requiring mature action (14:20). In the following passages, what other mature situations also require a mature response?

    a.   Rom. 16:17
    b.   Gal. 6:1–2
    c.   Eph. 4:11–13
    d.   Heb. 5:13–14
    e.   Heb. 13:17
    f.   James 3:1

3.) Does "When you assemble" in 14:26 refer to a worship service, Bible class, singing, lectureship, or … what? Is the emphasis on the conduct within an assembly (14:40), the reason for the assembly itself, or something else? Please explain.

4.) Why is the "women keeping silent" issue (14:34–35) so controversial and (thus) difficult to talk about? (There are several possible answers.) Do you think the Corinthians had the same reaction to Paul's instructions concerning women that many Christians have today? Why or why not?

Lesson Nineteen:

The Necessity of Christ's Resurrection (15:1–19)

The Proof of Christ's Resurrection (15:1–11): Paul shifts again to another topic of controversy: the resurrection of Christ. Some Corinthians were concerned that Christ had not really been resurrected. This teaching undermines the entire gospel, which is why Paul deals so directly with and lengthily on this subject.[137] We still have misunderstandings today concerning the resurrection (Christ's and ours), so this remains a subject worthy of our attention.

Paul begins by reminding what he had already taught the Corinthians (15:1–2). There is a measure of reproof in this, even a hint of exasperation. It is as if he is saying, "We *talked* about this when I was with you—and you all *believed* it! So now, what happened?!" He recaps what they already should have known:

- ❏ **First,** the gospel was *preached* to them. Paul did communicate to them a truthful message—he was not remiss in this. This gospel message necessarily included the resurrection of Christ; the two things—the message and Christ's resurrection—are inseparable.
- ❏ **Second,** the Corinthians *received* what Paul had preached—they were not passive listeners but active participants and willing recipients. This also makes them responsible to that which they have received. In essence, Paul says, "It was a true gospel—and you yourselves affirmed this when you believed in it."
- ❏ **Third,** they now *stand* in this gospel that they received—it has become their foundational belief system (2 Cor. 5:14–15).
- ❏ **Fourth,** they are *saved* by this gospel—that which necessarily includes Christ's resurrection from the dead. To deny the resurrection is to deny their own salvation.
- ❏ **Fifth,** this belief system will only work for them *if* they continue in it. God does not guarantee its promises apart from their personal faith; in the absence of that faith, a person forfeits everything (Col. 1:19–23).

❑ **Sixth,** all is useless if indeed they "believed in vain [or, to no purpose]" (15:2). This would be the case if the Corinthians were not honest about their conversion and/or the gospel was false. Christianity rests upon Christ's resurrection and hopelessly fails without it. Yet, Paul will go on to show that the problem here is not the gospel's authenticity but the Corinthians' wavering conviction.

Paul faithfully and accurately "delivered" to the Corinthians what he himself "received" from the Lord by way of revelation (15:3–4; see Gal. 1:11–12). The message he delivered is that Christ "died for our sins"[138] (1 Peter 3:18), was buried (Mark 15:42–46), and was resurrected "on the third day" (Mat. 12:38–40, 16:21). These things are of "first importance [lit., among the first]" since all else hinges upon them. There is no point in talking about the rest of the gospel if its *foundational teachings* are not true.[139] Incidentally, resurrection is not a mere resuscitation (or revival of life); it is not reincarnation, which is taught nowhere in Scripture. Resurrection is the return of one's spirit to his deceased body, as in the case of Lazarus (John 11:38–44) and Jesus (Mat. 28:5–6, Luke 24:36–43, etc.).

Many Greeks, however, had a very dim view of an afterlife. "For the Greeks, immortality lay precisely in getting rid of the body. For them, the resurrection of the body was unthinkable. Personal immortality did not really exist, because that which gave life was absorbed again in [their perception of] God, the source of all life."[140] In fact, the idea of a person's body being resurrected from the dead incited public ridicule, as what Paul faced in Athens (Acts 17:32).

Other Corinthians conceded that Christ was raised from the dead but believed that no one else could be. Paul's argument, however, presents an all–or–nothing doctrine: there either *is* or is *not* a resurrection of the dead. It is inconsistent and therefore illogical to preach Christ's bodily resurrection from the dead but not that of anyone else. The same Christ who walked out of *His* tomb promised to call everyone else out of *their* tombs (John 5:28–29). To verify His own resurrection, Christ appeared to various people who would serve as credible eyewitnesses of this event (15:5–8; see Acts 1:21–22, 5:30–32, etc.)—many more than were required for legal corroboration (2 Cor. 13:1).

Paul thought lowly of himself because he had persecuted the church (15:9) and was responsible for the deaths of some early believers (Acts 9:1–2, 22:4–5, and 26:9–11). Even so, he considered his apostolic authority equal to that of "the twelve" (see 2 Cor. 11:5). "But by the grace of God I am what I am ... " (15:10)—he did not credit himself with his choice to become an apostle but gave all credit to God (compare 1 Tim. 1:12–16). In any case, all the men Paul cited above preached the message of Christ's resurrection—the same message that the Corinthians heard from Paul and believed to be true (15:11). This entire passage:

- ❏ is a complete summary of Christ's atoning death and resurrection.
- ❏ refers to incidents which are not mentioned in the Gospels.
- ❏ declares that the death and resurrection of Christ were subjects embedded in the ancient prophecies.
- ❏ shows the force of the evidence on which the apostles relied and the number of living eyewitnesses to whom they could appeal.
- ❏ is [possibly] the earliest written testimony to the resurrection, written within only 25 years of that event.
- ❏ provides evidence that the resurrection of Christ is a literal, historical, and objective fact, and thus is "sufficient to convince the ... contemporary observer."[141]

The Necessity of the Resurrection (15:12–19): Despite all this, there were some within (or, influencing) the Corinthian church saying that "there is no resurrection of the dead" (15:12). Paul presents this as an incredulous position; he has already refuted such preaching (15:1–11):

- ❏ This (non–resurrection) is *not what happened*—it has no historical credibility or support.
- ❏ This is not what *the apostles of Christ* preach—because it is not what happened *and* is not what Christ Himself proved to be true.
- ❏ This is *not* the gospel of Christ—and those who claim it are self-condemned (Gal. 1:8).
- ❏ This is *not* "according to the Scriptures"—it has no basis in the word of God that was revealed through the prophets by the Holy Spirit (1 John 5:9–10).

- This is *not* verifiable through eyewitnesses but just the opposite is true.
- God cannot extend *life–giving grace* through a *dead Savior.*

Other negative and spiritually disastrous implications of a gospel that does not include a risen Savior include (15:13–19):

- This would invalidate *everything else* that Christ had promised: if He could not lay down His life *and* take it up again, He really does *not* have divine authority (John 10:17–18). Given this, all His other claims are immediately suspect (Eph. 1:18–23).[142]
- This would make *liars* of all those who *do* preach a resurrected Christ since they falsely testify that God *has* done what He did not (or could not) do.
- This would invalidate *everyone's redemption from sin* since no one can be redeemed apart from Christ (John 8:24, 14:6), and no redemption can be made unless Christ entered the heavenly tabernacle after being raised from the dead (Heb. 9:11–12).
- This would mean *no one is saved* and there is no hope for the living *or* the dead (1 Thess. 4:13–16). Thus, "we are of all men most to be pitied" (15:19) for having believed in a false gospel as though it were true and have nothing to look forward to.

Those who doubt (or refute) the resurrection of Christ do not realize the full implications of their case. "Unless these doubters are ready to accept these necessary deductions, they are forced to drop their proposition or to alter it so that those deductions do not follow."[143]

Questions

1.) Paul declared that the death, burial, and resurrection of Christ are of "first importance" in the preaching of the gospel. Are these typically of "first importance" in *today's* preaching of the gospel? If not, then what often *is*—and why?

2.) Did Paul's former persecution of the church (15:9–10) render him an ineffective witness for the resurrection of Christ? Please explain.

3.) If Christ claimed that He would raise from the dead (Mat. 16:21, John 10:14–18), and then *did so* (Mat. 28:6), what does this say about all else that He promised to do?

Lesson Twenty:

The Future Resurrection
(15:20–58)

Christ, the "First Fruits" of a Future Resurrection (15:20–28): "But now Christ has been raised … " (15:20)—Paul asserts this no longer as a possibility but as a historical and theological fact. Christ leads the way for all future resurrections: He is the "first fruits," and the resurrection of the faithful will be the harvest.[144] He is no longer dead and thus is superior to all those who *have* died (the meaning of "asleep" here). Since He rose from the dead, He can impart life to all who are *in* Him (Rom. 8:10–11).

Physical death is the result of a curse that God placed upon Adam, the ancestor of the entire human race (15:21; see Gen. 3:17–19). In "Adam"— used literally (the man himself) and representatively (as the ancestor of all men)—all "die," being under this curse. Christ, in His resurrection from the dead, overcame the curse. Ultimately, all of Adam's posterity will follow in his footsteps and "fall" from his or her innocence. In contrast, all who are "in Christ" will be "made alive" (15:22). While "made alive" can have a spiritual context (as in Eph. 2:4–5), here Paul refers to our physical resurrection from the dead. Just as Jesus was resurrected from His grave, so we will be from ours (John 5:28–29).

> **Adam → sin → curse upon humanity → our bodily death**
> **Christ → righteousness → overcame curse → promise of our bodily resurrection**

Just as God created the world in a purposeful and systematic order, so His salvation is purposeful and systematic. The doctrine concerning salvation and the future resurrection is not a chaotic mass of confusing doctrines and events, as often depicted today. God's plan will be carried out "each in his own order" (15:23): first, Christ's resurrection; second, His ascension to heaven [implied]; third, the resurrection of the faithful when He returns (1 Thess. 4:13–17); fourth, the ascension of those who remain alive (15:51–

53); fifth, "then comes the end" (15:24)—i.e., the end of time, the physical world (2 Peter 3:7, 10), and all opportunity for salvation.

After all things have run their course, Christ will hand the kingdom back to His Father (15:24). God gave His Son authority to rule over His kingdom a particular purpose, and His handing it *back* indicates that that He (Christ) had fulfilled that purpose. Christ took His seat at the right hand of God to begin this purpose (in His name) and to build His church (Mat. 28:18–19, Acts 2:33, etc.). But there is only a limited opportunity to submit to His authority and thus become a member of His church. When "the end" comes, all those called by His gospel either will have responded or refused to respond, and no further preaching of the gospel will bring about a different result. Christ's role as Mediator, Redeemer, and Savior will also have run its full course, for God would never call an end to it otherwise.

Another aspect to consider here is the abolition of "all rule and all authority and power" (15:24). This refers to the full subjection of every authority on earth as well as those in heaven—i.e., among men as well as whatever exists in the spiritual realm (see Col. 1:15–17). God the Father will bring about this subjection (according to the prophecy in Psalm 110:1) but it might be said that this will be carried out through His Son's authority in His capacity as the King over the Father's kingdom (15:25). In any case, "the end" will see the full and absolute subjection of every power that exists in the created world (visible and invisible), and *all* will answer to Christ (Phil. 2:9–11).

These powers ("enemies") are all people, entities, and governments that have defied Christ's authority and stand in opposition to Him. The last enemy is death itself (15:26): this speaks of the final abolition of human death since no one will face it any longer. John's *Revelation* fills in the blanks here: God will summon all who are alive *and* those who have died to appear before Him in the great Judgment Day (Rev. 20:11–15). Following this, all souls that had opposed Christ will be cast into the outer darkness; all who have obeyed Him will be welcomed into the holy and eternal city of God.

Paul adds a clarification to all of this (15:27–28): the Father having "put all things in subjection under His [Christ's] feet" (cited from Psalm 8:6) does not mean that He *relinquished* His authority *as* the Father. In having His Son reign over His kingdom, the Father retained His full sovereignty. In other words, Paul does not want the Corinthians (or us) to think that God stepped *down* from His throne for His Son to *ascend* it. Rather, Christ reigns at the right hand of God (Heb. 1:3, 8:1, 10:12, and 12:2) and remains—even as the King—in subjection to His Father (recall 11:3).

The Sin of Rejecting the Resurrection (15:29–34): We cannot separate 15:29–34 from what Paul has already said in 15:12–19. (It is characteristic of Paul to leave a thought for a moment to expound upon a related one and then return to his original thought.) In this way, 15:20–28 is parenthetical in design, and explains the "Otherwise" shift in discussion. Since this is true, "baptism for [or, with regard to] the dead" (15:29) alludes directly to one's conversion (symbolized by baptism in water) in hope of his resurrection from the dead. If the dead are not raised, then not even Christ has been raised (recall 15:13–14), rendering baptism meaningless. So then, Paul asks rhetorically, in essence: "Why should anyone be baptized (as were those who have since died in Christ) if there is no hope of being raised?"[145]

If there is no resurrection, it makes no sense why Paul is putting himself "in danger every hour" (15:30). Paul continues to show the absurdity of non–resurrection teaching (15:30). To paraphrase him: "Why am I purposely putting myself at risk by preaching the resurrection of Christ if indeed *there is no resurrection?*" As it is, Paul faced death "daily" for preaching a resurrected Christ (15:31); the fact that he endured such persecution is further evidence that he believes this to be true. It would be insane to do this from mere "human motives"; such sacrifices are only of "profit" for a gospel that transcends human motives, human abilities, and the grave itself. "If the dead are not raised, let us eat and drink, for tomorrow we die" (15:32)—i.e., let us not waste time preaching a false gospel (recall 15:14) but let us enjoy the pleasures of this life as much as possible, for once we die, we will be *without hope* of ever living again.

"Do not be deceived … " (15:33)—this is another way of telling the Corinthians that they *are* being deceived by some. "[B]ad company" [KJV, "evil communications"] here refers to those who have preached the false teaching of a non–resurrection. In general, however, it can refer to *any* "bad company"—i.e., any spiritual fellowship with those posing as Christians but who promote doctrines that contradict sound apostolic teaching (2 John 1:9–11). "Become sober–minded … and stop sinning" (15:34)—Paul links the incorrect teaching of the resurrection with having "no knowledge of God." This is a strong and well–deserved rebuke. The Corinthians prided themselves on being wise, yet their having embraced this teaching exhibited a gross ignorance of God and His doctrine.

The Nature of the Resurrected Body (15:35–49): In this next section, Paul seems to be purposely wordy and repetitive because he does not want to be misunderstood; the Corinthians are child–like in some of their spiritual thinking, and thus require child–like explanations (recall 3:1–2); and this is a difficult subject to begin with, since it deals with something (i.e., bodily resurrection) perplexing to human understanding. In fact, he speaks of things that lay outside the realm of every natural expectation. On the other hand, what Paul says is not meant to be a scientific treatise on the resurrected body, only a factual confirmation that there will *be* a bodily resurrection.

Some of the controversy over the resurrection stemmed from the difficulty of imagining a resurrected human body (15:35). Paul boldly calls the Corinthians "fools" when they wrongly assume that the resurrected body will be exactly like our human, earthly, mortal bodies. "That which you sow" cannot compare to what it becomes. This is just as true for the seed of a plant (John 12:23–24) as it is for a human body (15:36–37). Just as God "gives … a body" in place of (or, as a transformation of) the seed, so He gives a new form to the human body that is put into the ground (15:38). Likewise, just as earthly bodies (of men, beasts, birds, and fish) are different in composition, so there is a different composition for the resurrected body (15:39). Likewise, just as there are different "glories" in the earthly realm, which vary from form to form (e.g., star to star) as well as from class to class (e.g., sun to moon), so there will be another *kind* of glory for the resurrected body (15:40–42a).

In other words, one cannot appraise what is spiritual by what is "natural" or earthly (recall 2:12–15). This is not to say that the resurrected body has no definite form at all (2 Cor. 5:1–4) but that it will be *different* from that which was "sown." Whereas the human body is "natural," "perishable," "sown in dishonor," and "sown in weakness," the resurrected body is raised *without* these characteristics (15:42b–44a). Such language describes the natural human body that has been corrupted with sin *and* is incapable of overcoming the world on its own.

Furthermore, the fact that there *is* a "living [human] body," there must be a "spiritual [human] body" that corresponds, complements, and animates that physical body (15:44b). We see this in Christ's own resurrection: He was recognizable *as* Jesus, though His body no longer conformed to the physical world as it did previously. Thus, the Person laid *in* the tomb was the same One who came forth *from* the tomb. Just as Jesus called Lazarus forth from the tomb with His voice (John 11:43), so He will call "*all* who are in the tombs" to *come out of the tombs* (John 5:28–29, emphasis added).

People continue to grapple with this subject. They question how those who have been dead for so long can live again, or how a thoroughly decomposed body can be reconstituted into a physical, human form. Such thinking imposes *natural* and *earthly processes* upon a *supernatural* and *omnipotent God*. The same God who formed Adam from the dust of the earth and breathed into him the breath of life (Gen. 2:7) is certainly capable of doing this for all those who followed Adam. Such things defy natural laws, science, and expectations; they are contrary to everything we observe in this world; one is just as unnatural as the other. And yet, "with God all things are possible" (Mat. 19:26). While Adam became the *recipient* of life, Jesus Christ ("the last Adam") is the *giver* of life (15:45; recall 15:22).

"However, the spiritual is not first, but the natural" (15:46)—this is true for all human life. Adam, as a physical human being, preceded (in chronological time and earthly existence) the incarnation of Christ; likewise, our human, earthly existence precedes our resurrected, spiritual life. Our "first" composition is "earthy" [lit., made of dust]; our "second" (in time) composition is "from heaven" (15:47), or simply, of a spiritual nature. The earthy and the heavenly are not the same states of being or interchangeable (15:48). Yet, because we have already become one (earthy), so we—in the context of those who are in Christ and remain faithful to Him—will partake of the other (15:49).

A "Change" Is Necessary (15:50–58): While there is a relationship between the earthy body and the resurrected body, these remain incompatible and non–interchangeable. "[F]lesh and blood"—the constitution of our physical body—cannot "inherit" (or, obtain by way of inheritance) the spiritual reality of the kingdom of God (15:50). Likewise, the "perishable [or, incorruptible]" cannot participate in the heavenly realm in which there is no time, human bodies, or death. On the other hand—something Paul reveals in 2 Cor. 5:1–4—we *will* have a body in the spiritual realm. This body will not be exactly like the one we have now but will be perfectly fitted for life in God's world. This leaves many questions unanswered, to be sure, but Paul's purpose is not to detail that future body but only to say that we will *have* one.

All this is what the Corinthians should have known already through Paul's previous teaching on the matter as well as their own intuitive deduction—especially if they were as wise as they claimed. But now, Paul tells them something they did not know and *could not* have known intuitively—a "mystery" God revealed to him, and he now reveals to them (15:51–53):

- ❑ First, "we will not all sleep"—i.e., not all believers will be dead at the time of Christ's coming (already implied: recall 11:26 and 15:23); many will therefore never experience physical death.
- ❑ Second, "we will all be changed"—i.e., not only will God transform those resurrected from the dead, but He will also transform those who are alive at His coming.
- ❑ Third, this change or transformation will occur very quickly—in the blink ("twinkling") of an eye. God's power does not need vast amounts of time to produce profound and monumental change. If He can (and did) heal people instantaneously (e.g., Mark 1:42), then He can change the human body into a glorified one in the same amount of time. Time itself presents no hindrance or limitation to an all–powerful God who exists outside of physical time and space.
- ❑ Fourth, this change will happen "at the last trumpet"—a trumpet blast symbolizes a special call to attention, a time for gathering, or any momentous occasion (Num. 10:1–10, Josh. 6:4–9, etc.). Christ will announce His Second Coming clearly, unmistakably, and *loudly* "with a shout, with the voice of the archangel and with the trumpet of God" (1 Thess. 4:16).

- Fifth, "the dead will be raised"—an event that Jesus Himself promised *and* will oversee (John 5:28–29). The faithful who are alive will be transformed during the same event as the faithful who had died. (Specifically, the dead will be raised *first*; see 1 Thess. 4:13–17. However, Paul does not speak here of a specific order, only of the same event.) Physical death is not the end of our bodily existence or our conscious awareness. Furthermore, the same person that went *into* the grave will come *out* of it.

- Sixth, the dead will be raised "imperishable"—in its most basic sense, this means never to have to experience human or physical death again, the same meaning as "immortal." Those who are not in Christ or who have been unfaithful to their covenant with God remain outside of Paul's discussion.

- Seventh, "we will be changed"—the "we" here includes those who are alive at His coming as well as those who have been raised from the dead at His coming: *all* will be changed. The change refers to the miraculous transformation of a flesh–and–blood body into an incorruptible, immortal, and heavenly body (Phil. 3:20–21, 1 John 3:2). Below is a comparison of passages on this subject (emphases added):

John 11:25–26	1 Cor. 15:50–52	1 Thess. 4:15–17
Jesus said to her, "I am the resurrection and the life; he who believes in Me will live even if he dies, and **everyone who lives and believes in Me will never die.** Do you believe this?"	Now I say this, brethren, that flesh and blood cannot inherit the kingdom of God; nor does the perishable inherit the imperishable. Behold, I tell you a mystery; **we will not all sleep, but we will all be changed, in a moment, in the twinkling of an eye, at the last trumpet;** for the trumpet will sound, and the dead will be raised imperishable, and we will be changed.	For this we say to you by the word of the Lord, that we who are alive and remain until the coming of the Lord, will not precede those who have fallen asleep. For the Lord Himself will descend from heaven with a shout, with the voice of the archangel and with the trumpet of God, and the dead in Christ will rise first. **Then we who are alive and remain will be caught up together with them in the clouds to meet the Lord in the air, and so we shall always be with the Lord.**

Once the "perishable" is made "imperishable," then "Death is swallowed up in victory" (15:54; quoted from Isa. 25:8). Death is the result of the curse God had placed upon humankind because of sin; Christ's own resurrection *and* the resurrection of all who are faithful to Him will signify the utter destruction of death. The "victory" of death—in having claimed all those who have succumbed to it—will be robbed by the infinitely greater victory of resurrection from the grave (Eph. 4:8). Those redeemed will no longer feel the "sting" of death (15:55); those who are forever with the Lord will never face or fear death again.[146] The "sting" (or cause) of death is sin (15:56): human sin is the reason for all physical death. "The power of sin is the law" does not mean that God's law *leads* us to sin or ever endorses it. Rather, it means that law is what defines sin for what it is, and the violation of law produces the fear of guilt, judgment, and punishment (see Rom. 7:7–12,

Gal. 3:19–22, and Heb. 2:14–15). "If there were no sin, there would be no death. Man's transgression of the law gives death its lawful power."[147]

It is not *our* power or authority that brings about victory over sin, death, and the grave but *Christ's* (15:57). He is the One who walked out of His own tomb without any human mediation; He is the One who has overcome the world (John 16:33); He fulfilled the Father's "eternal purpose" (Eph. 3:11), not us. Even so, we can claim victory *through* Him if indeed we have been raised with Him in baptism and then remained faithful to Him until death (Rom. 6:4–10). "Therefore"—since all these things are so—the Corinthians have every reason to remain grounded in their faith and carry out the business of the kingdom (15:58). All such work, perseverance, and sacrifices will be worthwhile, given what lies ahead of them.

Questions

1.) Why is the Father "excepted" from the authority of Christ (15:27–28)? What does this say of the Father's *own* authority? Of Christ's submission to the Father (recall 11:3)?

2.) In 15:42–44, Paul spoke of those whom Christ will resurrect to glory. But this refers only to those who died in faith to Him. What of those who died outside of Christ? Or those who failed to remain faithful to Him? (See John 5:28–29, Acts 24:14–15, and 2 Thess. 1:6–10.)

3.) Why do you suppose Christ will resurrect our bodies from the grave in the first place? Is there a link between our resurrection and Christ's resurrection?

4.) Given this chapter, why is it *profitable* for us to "be steadfast, immovable, always abounding in the work of the Lord" (15:58)? How can we *know* that our "toil in the Lord" will not be "in vain"?

Lesson Twenty-one:

Closing Comments and Salutations (16:1–24)

Instructions Concerning the Collection (16:1–4): Paul wrote this epistle while he was in Ephesus, and he will stay there until Pentecost (see 16:8). After this, his plan is to travel his usual northwesterly route through Troas, then cross the Aegean Sea to Philippi in Macedonia, then south into Achaia where he would stay three months with the Corinthians. After this, he will make a brief stop at Ephesus (really, at nearby Miletus), and arrive in Jerusalem for the *following* Pentecost (Acts 20:1–6, 13–16). In other words, Pentecost mentioned in Acts 20:16 is a year later than the one mentioned here. Such is the time–consuming means of travel in the ancient world.

The purpose for all this traveling is two–fold: first, to encourage the newly founded churches on this route; second, to collect money from the (predominantly) Gentile churches for a relief effort in Jerusalem. As Paul explains in Rom. 15, the Gentiles have benefited spiritually from the Jewish Christians; therefore, Jewish Christians in need should be able to receive material (monetary) assistance from them. Paul does not hesitate to lay the responsibility of taking care of saints in need upon the brotherhood (2 Cor. 8:12–15).

All this identifies "the collection for the saints" (16:1–2). This collection is well–known, and in the present case is one about which the Corinthians had asked some questions.[148] Paul's instruction for how this money is to be collected is no different than what has been given to the churches in Galatia (although such instruction was not included in his letter to them). He does not want to collect money when he arrives; this can be done much more efficiently ahead of time.

The "first day of the week" is when the church normally assembles (Acts 20:7) and is also a most appropriate occasion for one to "put aside" for God his personal sacrifice. "[A]s he may prosper" means that there is no binding law to dictate the exact amount of this offering (2 Cor. 8:8, 9:6–9).[149] Once the money is collected, the Corinthians can send it to Jerusalem with someone of whom they approve, or this person can journey with Paul (and his entourage) to Jerusalem if he decided to go—which he ultimately did decide to do (16:3–4). The historical narrative of Paul's journey to Jerusalem is in Acts 20:1–21:17.

Paul's Plans for Himself and Others (16:5–12): Paul's plan is to spend time with the Corinthians when he travels through Achaia on his way to Jerusalem (16:5–8); we find out later that he does indeed spend three months with them (Acts 20:3). Meanwhile, he plans to stay in Ephesus until Pentecost (springtime), since traveling during the winter is difficult, dangerous, and seldom done, especially by sea. All of this is, at this point, dependent upon what "the Lord permits," since God has altered his travel plans before (e.g., Acts 16:6–12). The "many adversaries" in Ephesus (16:9) refers to the Jewish resistance he had already encountered (Acts 19:9ff). Even so, there is "a wide door for effective service" in that city—reminding us that there is work to be done even amid difficult opposition.

Paul is sending Timothy to the Corinthians and asks them to give him their support (16:10–11). He has already sent Timothy and Erastus ahead of him to Macedonia (Acts 19:22); their plan is to travel south to Achaia (where Corinth is) after that. However, Apollos—the impressive orator who has great influence among the Corinthians—has his own schedule (16:12). Possibly, he is wise enough to stay away from the church's party politics concerning him (recall 1:12), if indeed he knows of these things. In other words, some men Paul dispatches here or there, while other men operate independently of him. Yet, *all* of them whom Paul commends are teaching the same gospel that he teaches with no rivalry or competition between them.

Final Instructions to the Corinthians (16:13–24): In any case, the Corinthians have a moral responsibility—to Christ, His gospel, and themselves—to be vigilant, stay the course, and not be seduced by any teaching that cannot be proven to have come from God (16:13–14). "Be on the alert" is the same language Paul later uses to warn the Ephesian elders (Acts 20:31). Numerous times Paul tells Christians to "stand firm" (Gal. 5:1,

Eph. 6:11–14, Phil. 1:27, 4:1, etc.); there is an allusion here to a soldier or sentry maintaining his post and not dropping his weapon and running away in fear at the sight of an enemy.

"[A]ct like men"—not as the effeminate, homosexual, and otherwise perverse society from which they came (recall 6:9–10) but as those who maintain their God–given charge over their marriages, households, and churches. Paul is speaking directly to the males (or male leadership) of the congregation here.[150] "[B]e strong" accompanies "stand firm" and "act like men": it is impossible to separate out these exhortations, in the context of Christian duty. Christians do not find moral strength independent of Christ but *through* Him (Eph. 3:14–21). "Let all you do … in love"—because: love is "the perfect bond of unity" (Col. 3:14) among believers; love never does any harm to anyone (Rom. 13:10); and love is the epitome of godly virtue (recall 13:1–7).

Stephanas, Fortunatus, and Achaicus may have been those who brought the letter from the Corinthians to Paul (the "concerning the things about which you wrote" references) (16:15–18). Stephanus and his household were "first fruits" of Achaia, meaning that they were among the first to be baptized into Christ, at least by Paul (recall 1:16). Paul tells the Corinthians to be "in subjection" to such men, and *all* who labor among the churches (elders, preachers, teachers, missionaries, etc.). This subjection means show them proper regard; treat them with respect and honor (1 Thess. 5:12–13); equip them with whatever they need to do their work (3 John 1:7–8). Such men are deserving of high regard simply because of the kind of work they are doing for the church(es) and Paul in particular.

"The churches of Asia" (16:19) refers to the several churches in the Roman province of Asia Minor and may include any of the seven churches mentioned in Revelation (Rev. 1:11) as well as Colossae and possibly others. Aquila and Prisca (a.k.a. Priscilla) is the same couple Paul had originally met in Corinth (Acts 18:1–3) and had "risked their own necks" for him on an occasion unknown to us (Rom. 16:3–4). "All the brethren greet you" (16:20a)—likely, this refers to the brethren of the Ephesian church where Paul is staying when he writes this letter.

"Holy kiss" (16:20b) indicates a social custom, like our handshakes but taken to a higher level: not a mere gesture of kindness but a *holy* gesture. Whatever the form of greeting, it is to be a *holy* one; Christians are to greet one another with expressions of purity and sincerity, emulating the holy conduct of Christ Himself. Paul ends his epistle with his own personal gesture: he signs it with his own hand (16:21; see 2 Thess. 3:17). Paul's remark here indicates that this letter was likely dictated (possibly to Sosthenes—recall 1:1); this is not without precedent (Rom. 16:22).

Paul's solemn charge to "love the Lord" (16:22)—and his pronouncement of a curse upon all who will *not*—is a fitting end to this epistle. The word "accursed" [Greek, *anathema*] means "devoted to destruction"[151] (recall 12:3). Paul uses this same word in Gal. 1:8 as a curse upon anyone who preaches a different gospel than what he has preached. To refuse to love the Lord carries the same awful curse as refusing to uphold His revealed word (and vice versa). "Maranatha" (16:22) is an Aramaic word meaning, "Our Lord, come!"—a call for God's righteous judgment to come upon the world and especially upon those who refuse to love the Lord.[152]

Paul ends this momentous letter—one that has been difficult to write and (he anticipates) will be difficult to receive—with Christian love and affection. Regardless of how much correction the Corinthians require, or how much spiritual maturity they lack, he regards them as "saints" and "beloved brethren" (recall 1:2 and 15:58) and confers upon them the grace of the Lord Jesus (16:23). It would be as improper for him to confer divine grace upon Christians who are not in good standing with the Lord as it would be to do this for those who are not even Christians. In addition to this, Paul gives his own personal sentiment for them in an expression that is found nowhere else in his epistles (16:24; but compare 2 Cor. 11:11).

Questions

1.) Was the collection mentioned in 16:1–2 taken up for the same *reason* as our collections today (see Acts 4:34–35, 11:29–30)?

    a.   Is Paul stating a *command* to give or is he regulating the *process* of giving?

    b.   Are *we* commanded to give, or are we *expected* to do so (see 2 Cor. 8:7–11)?

2.) Why did Paul tell the Corinthians to "act like men" (16:13)? What *had* they been acting like (recall 3:1–3, 14:20)? What are *we* supposed to act like (Titus 3:8, 1 Peter 2:15–16)?

3.) Paul instructed the Corinthians to "be in subjection to such men [as Stephanas and Fortunatus] and to everyone who helps in the work and labors" (16:16).

    a.   What does this "subjection" mean—and how were they to practice this (see 1 Thess. 5:12–13)?

    b.   Are we still to "be in subjection" to workers and laborers in the church today? Who might these people be? What does this subjection look like?

❖END❖

Sources Used for This Study

Barclay, William. *Letters to the Corinthians.* Louisville, KY: Westminster John Knox Press, 1975, 2002.

Barnes, Albert. "1 Corinthians." *Barnes' Notes,* vol 11. Grand Rapids: Baker Book House, no date (orig. published in 1885 by Blackie & Sons in London).

Barrett, C. K. *The First Epistle to the Corinthians.* Peabody, MA: Hendrickson Publishers, 1996.

Conybeare, W. J. and J. S. Howson. *The Life and Epistles of St. Paul.* Grand Rapids: Eerdmans Publishing, 1964.

Coffman, James Burton. *Commentary on 1 and 2 Corinthians.* Austin, TX: Firm Foundation, 1977.

DeHaan, M. R. *Studies in First Corinthians.* Grand Rapids: Zondervan Publishing House, 1956.

Farrar, F. W. "1 Corinthians." *The Pulpit Commentary,* vol. 19 (H. D. M. Spence and Joseph Exell, eds.). Peabody, MA: Hendrickson Publishers, no date.

Grosheide, F. W. *The First Epistle to the Corinthians.* Grand Rapids: Eerdmans Publishing Co., 1953.

Hodge, Charles. *A Commentary on 1 Corinthians* (electronic edition). Database © 2004 by WORDsearch Corp.

Jamieson, Robert, Andrew Fausset and David Brown. *Commentary Critical and Explanatory on the Whole Bible (1871)* (electronic edition). Database © 2012 by WORDsearch Corp.

Kistemaker, Simon J. *New Testament Commentary: 1 Corinthians.* Grand Rapids: Baker Books, 1993.

Lenski, R. C. H. *Commentary on the New Testament: 1–2 Corinthians.* Peabody, MA: Hendrickson Publishers, 1998.

McGarvey, J. W., and Philip Y. Pendleton. *The Standard Bible Commentary: Thessalonians, Corinthians, Galatians and Romans.* Cincinnati, OH: The Standard Publishing Foundation, 1916.

McGuiggan, Jim. *Looking into the Bible Series: The Book of 1 Corinthians.* Lubbock, TX: Montex Publishing Co., 1984.

NASB Greek–Hebrew Dictionary (electronic edition). Robert L. Thomas, gen. ed.; updated by W. Don Wilkins. © 1981, 1988 by The Lockman Foundation (Anaheim, CA: Foundation Publications).

Robertson, A. T. *Word Pictures in the New Testament,* vol. 4. Grand Rapids: Baker Book House (no date); © 1931 by Sunday School Board of the Southern Baptist Convention.

Strong, James. *Strong's Talking Greek–Hebrew Dictionary* (electronic edition). © WORDsearch Corp., no date.

The Zondervan Pictorial Encyclopedia of the Bible, vol. 1. Merrill C. Tenney, gen. ed. Grand Rapids: Zondervan Publishing, 1976. Articles cited: A. Rupprecht, "Corinth"; F. F. Bruce, "Corinthians, First Epistle to the."

Willis, Mike. *A Commentary on Paul's First Epistle to the Corinthians.* Fairmount, IN: Cogdill Foundation, 1979.

Vincent, Marvin R. *Vincent's Word Studies* (electronic edition). Database © 2014 by WORDsearch Corp.

Vine, W. E. *Expository Dictionary of New Testament Words* (STBC; orig. 1952).

Endnotes

1   The idea of digging a canal between the two bodies of water had been around since the time of Julius Caesar. No one completed such a canal, however, until French engineers constructed one in the late 19th century (Simon J. Kistemaker, *New Testament Commentary: 1 Corinthians* [Grand Rapids: Baker Books, 1993]), 3–4.

2   "Its wealth was derived from its commercial traffic by sea and by land, its pottery and brass industries, and its political importance as the capital of Achaia [Greece]. At its height it probably had a population of 200,000 free men and 500,000 slaves" (A. Rupprecht, "Corinth," *The Zondervan Pictorial Encyclopedia of the Bible,* vol. 1, Merrill. C. Tenney, gen. ed. [Grand Rapids: Regency Reference Library, 1976], 961).

3   "There were attached [to the temple of Aphrodite] 1,000 priestesses who were sacred prostitutes, and in the evenings they came down from the Acropolis and plied their trade on the streets of Corinth. ... Corinth became a synonym not only for wealth, luxury, drunkenness and debauchery, but also for filth" (William Barclay, *Letters to the Corinthians* [Louisville, KY: Westminster John Knox Press, 1975, 2002], 3; bracketed words are mine).

4   "Even the most radical critics of today will not challenge either the canonicity or authenticity of this book" (Mike Willis, *A Commentary on Paul's First Epistle to the Corinthians* [Fairmount, IN: Cogdill Foundation, 1979], vii).

5   F. F. Bruce, "Corinthians, First Epistle to the," *Zondervan Encyclopedia,* 972.

6   After Paul's epistles to the Corinthians, "The church reemerges into literary history at the close of the first century AD. In about the year 97, Clement of Rome wrote a letter, which survives, to the church. It reveals that the church was still vexed by many of the same problems about which Paul wrote to them" ("Corinth," *Zondervan Encyclopedia,* 964).

7   "The Corinthian church was a carnal church. Many of its members were but recently converted from paganism and found it difficult to separate themselves from their old life. As a result the epistle is largely corrective and exhortatory, rather than doctrinal. Paul severely condemns their carnal practices and childish sectarianism. ... It is almost completely occupied with

Christian conduct and behavior" (M. R. DeHaan, *Studies in First Corinthians* [Grand Rapids: Zondervan Publishing House, 1956], 5, 12).

8   W. J. Conybeare and J. S. Howson, *The Life and Epistles of St. Paul* (Grand Rapids: Eerdmans Publishing Co., 1964), 380; their citation is from 2 Cor. 11:28.

9   Willis, *Commentary*, 5.

10   James Strong, *Strong's Talking Greek–Hebrew Dictionary*, electronic edition (© WORDsearch Corp., no date), G40.

11   A. T. Robertson, *Word Pictures in the New Testament*, vol. 4 (Grand Rapids: Baker Book House, no date), 72.

12   Twice, Paul uses the word "brethren [brothers]" in this passage (1:10–11). "By the very use of the word, Paul does two things. First, he softens the rebuke which is given, not in any threatening way, bus as from one who has no other emotion than love. Second, it should have shown them how wrong their dissensions and divisions were. They were fellow Christians, and they should have lived in mutual love" (T. Beza, quoted in Barclay, *Letters*, 17).

13   Kistemaker says: "We would expect that she resided in Corinth, for the text implies that the Corinthians knew her. Also, the news concerning the factions originated there. Another possibility is that Chloe was a businesswoman who lived in Ephesus and that her employees (either slaves, freedmen, or members of her family) regularly traveled between Corinth and Ephesus and were fully acquainted with the church. Whether Chloe was a Christian cannot be determined" (*1 Corinthians*, 45).

14   The Greek can also be rendered here as a statement rather than a question: "Christ has been divided!" or "Christ is divided!"; "Some of the best expositors render [this] as an assertion [rather than a rhetorical question]" (Marvin R. Vincent, *Vincent's Word Studies*, electronic edition [© 2014 by WORDsearch Corp.], on 1:13; bracketed words are mine).

15   "The pride of Corinth showed itself largely in philosophical conceit, and the citizens who vaunted their superior intelligence were divided into sects, of whom Aristotle, Plato, Zeno, Epicurus, and later philosophers, were the heads. The church became inflated with this same intellectual vanity, and apparently sought to make Christianity the rival of philosophy by exalting her humble teachers to be heads of religio–philosophical sects, and rivals of

Christ himself" (J. W. McGarvey and Philip Y. Pendleton, *The Standard Bible Commentary: Thessalonians, Corinthians, Galatians, and Romans* [Cincinnati, OH: The Standard Publishing Co., 1916], 52). This same mentality is still manifested in churches today, whenever members boast about who baptized them, who their preacher is, or how many generations of Christians are in their church pedigree.

16   To use this passage (1:14–17) to refute the necessity of baptism for salvation is to ignore: its context, which has nothing to do with proving or disproving baptism; all the other NT passages that positively require such baptism (Acts 2:38, Rom. 6:3–7, Gal. 3:27, etc.); all the examples in Acts of those who were baptized after hearing the message of Christ (Acts 8:12, 35–38, 16:14–15, 25–34, 18:8, etc.); Paul's own personal baptism in response to divine instruction (Acts 9:18, 22:16); and Christ's own commandment regarding the making of disciples to Him (Mat. 28:19).

17   A parallel situation exists in John 4:1–2, where Jesus taught the baptism of John (the Baptist), even though He Himself was not conducting the baptisms.

18   Kistemaker, *1 Corinthians*, 51.

19   Paul quotes from Isa. 29:14—a prophecy made 700 years before "the cross" to show that God had orchestrated this scenario all along. Christ's crucifixion was no accident; He was not a victim of circumstance; He was not defeated by either the Romans or the Jews. Instead, everything happened according to "the predetermined plan and foreknowledge of God" (Acts 2:23).

20   Robert Jamieson, Andrew Fausset, and David Brown, *Commentary Critical and Explanatory on the Whole Bible*, electronic edition (database © 2012 by WORDsearch Corp.), on 1:22.

21   "Stumbling block" refers to a snare or device used to capture animals; literally, it is a trap–stick (Strong, *Dictionary* [electronic], G4625). Lenski translates it as "deathtrap," which is really what it is, since it "is fatal in its effects" (*Interpretation*, 66).

22   The "word of the cross" and "Christ crucified" are examples of a synecdoche: a literary device in which a group of subjects is included in the mention of only one of those subjects. Thus, when Paul refers to Christ's

crucifixion, he means everything necessarily related to it as well: blood of atonement; sacrifice; forgiveness; drawing near to God; etc. "He does not mean to say that every sermon was a description of the crucifixion of our Lord, but that all his teaching and preaching related to the atonement wrought by Christ upon the cross" (McGarvey and Pendleton, *TSBE*, 58).

23   "Lord of glory" (2:8) calls to mind the praises given to God in the Psalms (e.g., 24:10); compare also with NT expressions in Acts 7:2, Eph. 1:17, and James 2:1). "'Lord of glory' is a title of divinity. It means 'possessor of divine excellence.' ... The person crucified, therefore, was a divine person" (Hodge, *Commentary* [electronic], on 2:8). Paul's quote in 2:9 is from Isa. 64:4.

24   Jesus identifies as the "Word [Greek, *Logos*] of God" in John 1:1–3, 14, and 1 John 1:1–3. Jesus, in His divine nature, "is to God what man's word is to himself, the manifestation or expression of himself to those without [i.e., apart from] him" (JFB, *Commentary* [electronic], on John 1:1; emphasis is theirs; bracketed words are mine). Jesus, then, is the physical revelation of God's message to humankind.

25   For a full discussion on this, I strongly recommend my book, *The New Testament Pattern: God's Plan for Christians and Their Churches* (Spiritbuilding Publishers, 2023); go to www.spiritbuilding.com/chad.

26   "Natural" is from the Greek, *psuchikos* (Strong, *Dictionary* [electronic], G5591), and refers to a man whose heart and thoughts do not seek God's Spirit, and from whom God's Spirit is absent (see Rom. 8:6–9 for a good contrast). "The man, therefore, whose cognition of truth depends solely upon his natural insight is natural, as contrasted with the spiritual man to whom divine insight is imparted. In other words, the organ employed in the apprehension of spiritual truth characterizes the man. Paul therefore 'characterizes the man who is not yet capable of understanding divine wisdom ...'" (Vincent, *Word Studies* [electronic], on 2:14).

27   "[Calvinists] understand this verse to assert that man cannot understand the Scriptures until God operates on his heart," what they call "illumination" (Willis, *Commentary*, 80–81). But: the context does not at all support this; this is not what Paul says; and no one would believe such a conclusion unless he were trying to prove Calvinism (i.e., circular reasoning). For an overview of Calvinism, I recommend chapter 17 in

my book, *The Gospel of Saving Grace* (Waynesville, OH: Spiritbuilding Publishers, 2020); go to www.spiritbuilding.com/chad.

28 "Master builder" (or, "chief constructor") is from a single Greek word, *architekton* (from *arche*, "chief" + *tekton*, "craftsman"), from which we get our English word "architect" (Strong, *Dictionary* [electronic], G753).

29 Such is the insight of James MacKnight (as quoted in James B. Coffman, *Commentary on 1 and 2 Corinthians* [Austin, TX: Firm Foundation, 1977], 47), Mike Willis (109), and others.

30 The "you" in 3:16–17 must refer to the antecedent—i.e., the entire congregation; thus, it is used to denote the group, not an individual person. It is impossible for anyone to destroy Christ's body; it is entirely possible, however, to destroy a congregation.

31 Paul cites Job 5:13 and Psalm 94:11 to underscore his point and show that this has been the case since antiquity.

32 Lipscomb, *First Corinthians*, 57; bracketed words are mine.

33 "The term 'ministers' ['stewards'] here means under–rowers. The church is a ship, or galley; Christ is the chief navigator, or magisterium; and all the evangelists and teachers are mere oarsmen with no ambition to be leaders [on par with or instead of Christ]" (McGarvey and Pendleton, *TSBC*, 67; bracketed words are mine).

34 The NT sense of "having" a woman means, in other places, to be married; see Mat. 14:4, 22:28, 1 Cor. 7:2, and 7:29. We assume this man is married to his stepmother, since otherwise the woman would be identified as his mother, not "his father's wife." Because Paul says nothing about any church action toward this woman, she is likely not a Christian.

35 Strong, *Dictionary* (electronic), G4202. "*Porneia* is sometimes used (Acts 15:20, 29) of such sin in general and not merely of the unmarried whereas *moicheia* is technically adultery on the part of the married (Mark 7:21)" (Robertson, *Word Pictures*, 111).

36 The assumption that this man's father was dead "would make the case a little less horrible, yet would not eliminate its worst feature"—namely, that of incest (Lenski, *Interpretation*, 207).

37 McGarvey and Pendleton, *TSBC*, 72.

38   Adapted from Jim McGuiggan, *Looking into the Bible Series: The Book of 1 Corinthians* (Lubbock, TX: Montex Publishing Co., 1984), 62.

39   We have no instruction to disfellowship anyone in another congregation or from the entire brotherhood; such jurisdiction belongs only to Christ and His apostles. We must also recognize the limitation of our human judgments: we can cite God's authority, but we cannot assume or replace it. In other words, the possibility for human error always remains, despite our best intentions.

40   C. K. Barrett, *The First Epistle to the Corinthians* (Peabody, MA: Hendrickson Publishers, 1996), 133; bracketed word is mine.

41   In 5:12, Paul admitted that he did not "judge" those outside the church, yet here (6:2) he claims that "saints will judge the world." The context is completely different however: Paul has no right to personally condemn the world (same usage as in Mat. 7:1–2), but saints will participate in the judgment of the world as an example of what God expected of all men, if nothing else (same usage as in Mat. 12:41–42).

42   "There is a natural difference between the two tribunals which Paul contrasts. The pagan judges operate with legal power and machinery in a regular order of law or trial; when Christian brethren are asked to decide disputes they have no legal and police power and no legal machinery but serve voluntarily, operate with arbitration and the Christian sense of fairness, and rely on moral power for their results. But for all ordinary disputes between Christians, if these must be carried that far, the submission of the case to be tried by trusted brethren should certainly be preferred" (Lenski, *Interpretation*, 235).

43   Robertson, *Word Pictures*, 119.

44   It has been traditionally taught that the kingdom of God and the church the same. There is no doubt a necessary relationship between the two, but they are not interchangeable. Paul's usage of "the kingdom of God" refers to an inheritance that has not yet been received by faithful Christians, as well as something that will never be received by those who refuse or no longer want to live by faith in God. The righteous will inherit the kingdom, the unrighteous will not. Christ promises everyone who is in His church a future place in His eternal kingdom, if they live in such a way that is consistent with the nature and virtue of Christ the King.

45 Strong, *Dictionary* (electronic), G4205.

46 *Ibid.,* G1496.

47 Vincent, *Word Studies* (electronic), on 6:9. "The connection here seems to demand such an interpretation, as it occurs in the description of vices of the same class–sensual and corrupt indulgences. It is well known that this vice was common among the Greeks—and particularly prevailed at Corinth" (Albert Barnes, *Barnes' Notes,* vol. 11 [Grand Rapids: Baker Book House, no date], 101–102).

48 Barclay, *Letters,* 58; bracketed words are mine. Kistemaker translates this word here "homosexuals," and the next word "sodomites." There is a clear relationship between the two words. "The…Greek word, *malakoi* (homosexuals), relates to 'men and boys who allow themselves to be misused homosexually.' This word connotes passivity and submission" (Kistemaker, *1 Corinthians,* 188). In contrast, the next word [*arsenokoitai,* "sodomites"] "represents men who initiate homosexual practices (1 Tim. 1:10). They are the active partners in these pursuits" (*Ibid.*).

49 "In ancient Greece and Rome, few people were exclusively homosexual; but was a period of great sexual experimentation, and the bisexual lifestyle was considerably more common than most people today would imagine" (Barclay, *Letters,* 63).

50 Strong, *Dictionary* (electronic), G2812.

51 *Ibid.,* G3060.

52 *Ibid.,* G727.

53 Lipscomb, *First Corinthians,* 88.

54 In this understanding, "stomach" is differentiated from "body": the stomach is for food, but the need for both (stomach and food) will cease upon one's death. However, the "body" is still to be raised from the dead— not to eat and drink any longer, but as a demonstration of God's resurrective power (1 Cor. 15:35–49).

55 "No one in Paul's day would disagree with what he wrote. Though the Corinthians would admit this, some today would deny that one becomes one with a harlot through intercourse. The sex act is seen as simply a physical performance that does not affect one's personality. That is not true; the

fornicator becomes more and more like the harlot in thought and attitude as he persists in the sinful relationship" (Willis, *Commentary*, 200).

56   For further study on the indwelling of the Spirit, I recommend my book, *The Holy Spirit of God: A Biblical Perspective* (Spiritbuilding Publishers, 2010); go to www.spiritbuilding.com/chad.

57   "Two things characterize a temple. First, it is sacred as a place where God lives, and therefore it cannot be profaned with impunity. Second, the temple is not owned by man but by God. Both these things are true of the believer's body" (Hodge, *Commentary* [electronic], on 6:19–20).

58   Barrett, *Epistle*, 156. Regarding marital leadership, the husband is to be the "head" of his wife (Eph. 5:23); with regard to the sexual realm, the relationship is mutually shared and beneficial.

59   There may also be other reasons why widows, for example, ought to get married: see 1 Tim. 5:11–15.

60   It is important to notice that Paul never acknowledges a situation where a person is bound to a marriage from which his or her spouse has been "freed." Either the covenant of marriage exists between two people, or it does not exist at all.

61   People commonly assume Paul is here citing specifically what Jesus said (as recorded in Mat. 19:9 or Mark 10:11–12), but this is impossible to prove and necessary to maintain. Jesus spoke exclusively to Jews concerning their abuses or misunderstandings of the Law of Moses; Paul writes to a mixed audience that is under a covenant with God through Christ. Many also assume that Jesus (in the gospels) laid down church doctrine regarding marriage and divorce, but this also misrepresents His ministry to the Jews and His fulfillment of their covenant. And, many assume that Jesus changed whatever Moses taught in order to create church doctrine, but this undermines Jesus' sinless obedience to God as a law–keeper. No king of Israel ever had permission to change God's laws, but only to obey them (Deut. 17:19–20).

62   "Leave" [Greek, *chorizo*] means to place room between (two things), or simply to separate; "divorce" [Greek, *aphiemi*] means to put or send away (Strong, *Dictionary* [electronic], G5563 and G863, respectively).

63   While the Jews could divorce their wives only under a certain condition (Deut. 24:1), Jesus said that this provision was given only because of "the hardness of your heart" and was never God's intention "from the beginning" (Mat. 19:8). Christians who invoke the so–called adultery clause (of Mat. 19:9) to end their marriages fall into the same category: while this may be permissible, it is still not what God intended "from the beginning." What God wants is for those who make a serious mistake to own up to and repent of it, and beg their spouse's forgiveness, and for the defrauded spouse to be forgiving (Col. 3:13b). Even in the case of adultery, this is the ideal recourse, not divorce.

64   "[A]lthough the marriage bond cannot be dissolved by any human authority, because it is, in virtue of the law of God, a covenant for life between one man and one woman, yet it can be annulled—not rightfully, but effectually" (Hodge, *Commentary* [electronic], on 7:10–11).

65   It is an "abomination before the Lord" for a divorcee to remarry the husband that she abandoned once she becomes the spouse of another. Even though this injunction is given in the Law of Moses (Deut. 24:4), it speaks of a moral crime, not merely a ritual violation (like eating pork or failing to ceremonially cleanse oneself). The fact that it is not specifically repeated in the New Testament does not make it vanish altogether, any more than the sexual indecencies of Lev. 18:6–23 have vanished. Moral laws are consistent in all covenants with God.

66   Some argue here that "the marriage is not dissolved by her departing" (Willis, *Commentary*, 221), and thus if she marries a man other than the husband she abandoned, she allegedly commits adultery in the sex act of the second marriage. Yet, this forces words and actions into the text that are not necessarily implied. Furthermore, Paul says that, unless she reconciles with her husband, she is "unmarried." A person cannot be married and unmarried all at once. Likewise, she cannot have a husband with which to be reconciled unless she is still married. (There is no such thing as an unmarried husband or wife, any more than there is a "bachelor" who is a married man.)

67   The so–called "traditional" view of marriage and divorce says that a Christian that abandons her (or his) marriage nonetheless remains forever married to her first spouse. Yet, if she remains married, then so does her husband; a one–sided/–party marriage is foreign both to Scripture and real

life. Paul places the consequences of one's action on the person leaving the marriage, not the one who has been abandoned. Given this, in my opinion: permanent abandonment of the marriage constitutes its termination, regardless of whether sexual adultery has occurred. Paul is not punishing the one who was abandoned by putting him in perpetual limbo (a "married but without a wife" situation), but the one who did the abandoning. Repentance is required of the one leaving, not the one who is left behind. The very concept of marriage, and the terms and conditions of the covenant of marriage, are impossible to fulfill if one party has deserted that covenant.

68   Lenski, *Interpretation*, 290.

69   "Paul is thinking of the possibilities and probabilities of the unbeliever's being saved, so that the home can be kept together, and can be prevented from being broken up" (DeHaan, *Studies*, 82).

70   Christianity cannot, however, accommodate any sinful situation or relationship. For example, if a woman is cohabitating with a man outside of marriage, and then she wants to obey the gospel, she must remove herself from that immoral situation to join herself to the Lord (recall 6:17). However, if she is legitimately married to an unbeliever, she does not have to remove herself from that marriage to be spiritually joined to Christ.

71   I have written more extensively on the issue of slavery in my *Philippians, Colossians, and Philemon Commentary* (Spiritbuilding Publishers, 2024); go to www.spiritbuilding.com/chad. Regardless, I recommend the study of the following related passages: Eph. 6:5–8, Col. 3:22–25, 1 Tim. 6:1–2, Titus 2:9, and 1 Peter 2:18–20. It is conspicuous that Paul never condemns the institution of slavery itself, but only urges Christians who are slaves to conduct themselves in such a way that does not betray Christian doctrine.

72   "Virgins" in this context means both male and female virgins; later (7:36) he speaks specifically of females. By "virgins," Paul means those who have never been married.

73   "The woman who is unmarried, and the virgin …" (7:34) is a conspicuous phrase. All virgins are unmarried, but not all unmarried women are virgins. It is my opinion, for what it is worth, that the "unmarried" here refers to those who are divorced (recall comments on 7:10–11). It does not seem reasonable to assume that the "unmarried" here are widows, since Paul deals with this other class of women later (7:39–40).

74   Barnes, *Notes*, 132.

75   I have encountered Christians who are pointedly dogmatic on this verse, saying, in so many words, "It says what it says in plain English!" Yet, in 1 Cor. 8:1, Paul says to us in plain English that "Knowledge makes arrogant"—and yet everyone knows that not all people who have knowledge are immediately arrogant. And Jesus says, again in plain English, that "none of you can be My disciple who does not give up all his own possessions" (Luke 14:33)—and yet no one takes this to mean exactly what He says and thus gives up everything he has. My point is this: we need to study the Bible in context, rather than studying stand–alone verses chosen preferentially to prove a favored conclusion. The subject of marriage and divorce in Scripture is a difficult one, and will never be fully explained, understood, or resolved by any stand–alone verse.

76   This "in the Lord" expression is used repeatedly in Paul's writings to refer to those who are Christians; see, for example, Rom. 16:8–13, 1 Cor. 4:17, Eph. 2:21, 6:21, and Col. 4:7.

77   "What complicated matters still further was that, at this time, people believed strongly and fearfully in demons and devils. The air was full of them. They were always lurking to gain an entry into an individual; and, if they did, they would injure the body and unhinge the mind of the person entered. One of the special ways in which these spirits gained entry was through food: they settled on the food as people ate, and so got inside them. One of the ways of avoiding that was to dedicate the meat to some good god whose presence in the meat put up a barrier against the evil spirit. For that reason, nearly all animals were dedicated to a god before being slaughtered; and, if that was not done, as a defence [sic], meat was blessed in the name of a god before it was eaten. It therefore followed that it was almost impossible to eat meat at all which was not in some way connected with one of the popular gods. Could Christians eat it? That was the problem; and, clearly, although to us it may be merely a matter of historical interest, the fact remains that, to the Christians in Corinth or any other Greek city, it was a problem which pervaded all life, and which had to be settled one way or another" (Barclay, *Letters*, 85–86).

78   Paul's phrase "in heaven or on earth" speaks the point of view of those who believe in these gods, not their actual existence.

79 Even when this understanding is inaccurate, the willful violation itself is still sinful, since "whatever is not from faith is sin"—Rom. 14:23.

80 The word translated "dining" is from the Greek *katakeimai* (G2621); "Literally, [the word means] 'lying down,' according to the ancient custom of reclining on a couch at table" (Hodge, *Commentary* [electronic], on 8:10; bracketed words are mine). "The idol temples were frequently used as banqueting–houses; but for a Christian to feast in such a place was a reckless abuse of liberty" (McGarvey and Pendleton, *TSBC*, 86).

81 In our modern, hyper–sensitive, and politically correct society, the word "offended" has taken on a meaning that has nothing to do with what it means in Scripture. To "offend" someone, in the biblical context (which is often characterized as becoming a stumbling block to that person), is to sin against him in some way (Mat. 18:6–7, Rom. 14:13, 21). This indicates a moral crime, not a personal displeasure, a strong disagreement, or an emotional upsetting of some sort. On the other hand, if one is offended because he rejects God's revealed truth (as in Mat. 11:6, 13:57, Rom. 9:32–33, and 1 Cor. 1:23), despite all the proofs God offers to substantiate that truth, then this also is a moral crime. In such a case, the one who provided the truth is not guilty of any crime, but the sin lies with the one who rejected it.

82 McGarvey and Pendleton, *TSBC*, 88; bracketed words are mine.

83 Paul confirms, however, that all the other apostles are married, as well as the physical brothers of Christ (Mark 6:3), and in particular "Cephas" (a.k.a. Peter—John 1:42; see Mat. 8:14), whom the Jews might claim is a more legitimate apostle than Paul. His point is: they are no better than him for having married, nor is he any less than them for having chosen to remain unmarried. Coffman (based on J. W. McGarvey and others) believes that "eating," "drinking," and "taking a wife" here refers to a lifestyle based upon remuneration—i.e., the preacher (and his family) was supported by the church (*Commentary*, 130); "This is a plea for the support of the preacher's wife and children" (Robertson, *Word Pictures*, 142). If true, this may be the reason for Paul's reference to himself and Barnabas having to work to provide for themselves (9:6) rather than be remunerated by those to whom they preached. In essence, Paul appears to say: "Are we [himself and Barnabas] not worthy of compensation simply because we are not married and do not have a family to support?"

84   Barnabas was one of Paul's original traveling companions (Acts 13:1–3). At some point, they had a difficult separation (Acts 15:36–40). Incidentally, Paul's favorable mention of Barnabas here indicates that he still holds him in high regard, despite what happened earlier.

85   Barrett, *Epistle*, 200; Coffman, *Commentary*, 131.

86   "The ministry of preaching was not just a job with the apostle Paul. It was not another way of just making a living, just a profession, but it was a divine call, an imperative call, an inescapable responsibility. Paul was not a preacher by choice. He was a preacher by conviction" (DeHaan, *Studies*, 108).

87   Robertson, *Word Pictures,* 148.

88   This is exactly what Jesus did in every conversation with His challengers: He set aside His right to assert His full authority as the Son of God to win those who struggled with the message of the kingdom.

89   In this same way, the Philippians became fellow "partakers of grace" with Paul when they supported his preaching of it, even while he was in prison (Phil. 1:7); John was a "fellow partaker" of the many other Christians facing persecution when he himself suffered exile for his role as a witness of Christ (Rev. 1:9); and all of us will be fellow "partakers of Christ, if we hold fast the beginning of our assurance firm until the end" (Heb. 3:14).

90   "One of our greatest necessities is to learn the art of getting along with people; and so often the trouble is that we do not even try" (Barclay, *Letters*, 99).

91   Barnes, *Notes*, 169–171. "Of the Greek Athletic Festivals, the most famous was that held every fourth year at Olympia in the west of the Peloponnese [i.e., the peninsula in southern Greece which is connected to the mainland via the isthmus of Corinth]. Very famous and ancient also was the Isthmian festival held every two years at the Isthmus, about eight miles from, and in full view of, the city of Corinth" (Willis, *Commentary*, 309; bracketed words are mine).

92   "These are the words in which the instructors of the young in the exercise schools (*gymnasia*) and the spectators on the race course exhorted their pupils to stimulate them to put forth all exertions. The gymnasium was a prominent feature in every Greek city. Every candidate had to take

an oath that he had been ten months in training, and that he would violate none of the regulations (2 Tim. 2:5; compare 1 Tim. 4:7–8). He lived on a strict self–denying diet, refraining from wine and pleasant foods, and enduring cold and heat and most laborious discipline. The 'prize' awarded by the judge or umpire was a chaplet of green leaves; at the Isthmus, those of the indigenous pine, for which parsley leaves were temporarily substituted" (JFB, *Commentary* [electronic], on 9:24).

93   The Greek word here [*adokimos*] is often translated "reprobate" in the KJV. It is translated in the NASB as "depraved" (Rom. 1:28, 2 Tim. 3:8), "fail the test" (1 Cor. 13:5–6), "unapproved" (1 Cor. 13:7), "worthless" (Titus 1:16), and "rejected" (Heb. 6:8). Some commentators believe translators soften the word here in 9:27 so as not to conflict with Calvinism, which claims the "impossibility of apostasy" of the elect.

94   McGarvey and Pendleton, *TSBC*, 96.

95   Kistemaker, *1 Corinthians*, 323.

96   The "destroyer" refers to "an angel commissioned by God to use the pestilence as an instrument of destruction. Hence sometimes the destruction is ascribed to the plague, as in Numbers 14:14; sometimes to the angel, as here; and sometimes both the agent and the instrument are combined, as in 2 Samuel 24:16. See Acts 12:23" (Hodge, *Commentary* [electronic], on 10:10).

97   Strong, *Dictionary* (electronic), G3986.

98   JFB, *Commentary* (electronic), on 10:14; bracketed word is mine; emphasis is theirs.

99   "Demon" may not always refer to satanic angels, but (according to man–made religion) can also refer to disembodied spirits who served as intermediaries to the gods; see Acts 17:22, where "superstitious" literally means "demon–fearing." At the same time, "Demonology is a deep and dark subject here pictured by Paul as the explanation of a heathenism which is a departure from God (Rom. 1:19–23) and a substitute for the worship of God. It is a terrible indictment which is justified by the licentious worship associated with paganism then and now" (Robertson, *Word Pictures*, 156).

100 "What the apostle means to say is that there is not merely an incongruity and inconsistency between a person being the guest and

friend of Christ, and the guest and friend of evil spirits, but that the thing is impossible. It is as impossible as that the same man should be wicked and holy at the same time" (Hodge, *Commentary* [electronic], on 10:21).

101 Words like "profitable" and "edifying" must be defined by the context of Scripture, not according to one's own opinion or the consensus of those who stand to benefit personally from this action.

102 For a deeper study on "expediency," I strongly recommend my book, *The New Testament Pattern: God's Plan for Christians and Their Churches* (Spiritbuilding Publishers, 2023); go to www.spiritbuilding.com/chad.

103 "In theory Paul sided with the strong, but in sympathy he was one with the weak; yet he did not permit them [i.e., the weak] to exercise a vexatious tyranny over him because of their scruples" (McGarvey and Pendleton, *TSBC*, 107).

104 "The veil in all eastern countries was, and to a great extent still is, the symbol of modesty and subjection. For a woman to discard the veil in Corinth, therefore, was to renounce her claim to modesty, and to refuse to recognize her subordination to her husband. The apostle's whole argument in this paragraph is based on the assumption of this significance in the use of the veil" (Hodge, *Commentary* [electronic], on 11:2–16).

105 The English words "man" and "woman" here are translated from the exact same Greek words that are elsewhere translated "husband" and "wife" (*aner* and *gune*, respectively). It is the English translators who have decided for us how to render these terms, supposedly being based upon the context. But such decisions, while made by learned men, may be biased, or may not always properly or conclusively render the original thought of a given passage.

106 "The verse is meaningless unless women from time to time were moved, in the Christian assembly in Corinth, to pray and prophesy aloud and in public" (Barrett, *Epistle*, 250).

107 "The word also in this verse [11:6] plainly shows that the two veils— the natural hair and the veil with which the head was covered—are under consideration. If her head be not covered with a veil, let her hair be shorn" (J. W. Shepherd, in Lipscomb, *First Corinthians*, 164; bracketed citation is mine).

108 "Although the woman is given a place below the man, vs. 11 makes abundantly clear that she is not the slave of the man. Her inferior position is not because the man has a greater degree of dignity than she. ... [However,] the woman who is a creature of God [by virtue of the Creation] will have a position of honor, a position far better than that which Greek paganism was able to offer" (Grosheide, *Commentary*, 258; bracketed words are mine).

109 It is likely that the early Christians practiced so-called "love feasts"—shared meals, under the pretense of Christian fellowship, akin to our modern potlucks. This may be what is happening in Acts 2:46, for example, when fellow believers came together to talk of their faith and gained encouragement over a meal. This also led to abuses: first, the situation that Paul is dealing with here in 1 Cor. 11; secondly, those who used these occasions as a masquerade of Christian love, when in fact they had ulterior (likely, sensual or seductive) motives, as Jude implies (Jude 1:12).

110 Many times, Christian men presiding over the Lord's Supper fixate upon the great pain and suffering that Christ endured upon the cross, and that this is what we are to "remember." Many of our hymns only reinforce this idea. Yet, the NT writers hardly speak of this; in fact, the gospel writers only imply His suffering in what He endured (in His scourging, beating, and crucifixion itself). Instead, the NT writers often focus much more upon the reproach and abject humiliation that Christ endured for our sakes—not just in being crucified as a common criminal, but in having entered our spiritually-ignorant, sin-filled, and hopeless world to begin with (see Phil. 2:5–9). We should not just "remember" (as in, call to mind) that Jesus died pathetically upon a cross, but we should "remember" (as in, give our obedient worship to) the One who had laid aside His glory as a Divine Being so that He could rescue us from our own foolish defiance against our Creator.

111 Paul is not saying, "If you do not feel worthy, you should not partake of this." The fact is, none of us are ever worthy to worship Christ; we are made worthy through His body and blood—the very things being "remembered" in the Lord's Supper. On the other hand, if one is guilty of unrepented sin, then he contradicts his alleged commemoration of Christ's death—in this case, he should not partake because his heart is not right with God. We do not partake of the Lord's Supper to become justified; rather, we should seek justification first to partake.

112 *NASB Greek–Hebrew Dictionary* (electronic edition), Robert L. Thomas, gen. ed.; updated by W. Don Wilkins (© 1981, 1988 by The Lockman Foundation), G1384a.

113 "Sleep" has more than one meaning in the NT; compare, for example, 1 Thess. 4:13–14 and 5:6. It is context, not the mere definition of a word itself, that provides the correct usage of any given word or phrase in Scripture. In the present case (11:30), there is no reason for Paul to mean a literal sleep, as if some Corinthians were sleeping through the Lord's Supper or staying home to sleep instead of assembling together. Rather, it carries the meaning of physical death (John 11:11–14, Acts 7:60, and 1 Cor. 15:51). "[Paul] deems it necessary to inform the Corinthians that their illnesses and deaths are related to the verdict that God has handed down to them. This verdict stems from their improper observance of the Lord's Supper" (Kistemaker, *1 Corinthians*, 404). At least one commentator (Willis, *Commentary*, 405) believes that the sicknesses and deaths ("sleep") mentioned here are spiritual, not physical. However, his argument rests on his difficulty in accepting a divine punishment that would prevent one's possible repentance. God has already shown to punish His people with death (Acts 5:1–11), so it is not at all unreasonable to see it being manifested in the present situation.

114 Some have argued that this verse (11:33) prohibits a second offering of the Lord's Supper in a second Sunday service. While there are pros and cons to a second offering, Paul's words here are not to endorse or prohibit such a thing. In fact, this is not even under consideration. The problem of the Corinthians was that they were intentionally dividing themselves by status, economic standing, or other distinguishing factors. Those who come to a second service, being prevented by circumstances beyond their control to attend the first service, are not intentionally dividing themselves from the rest of us, nor are we doing so to them; this is a different matter altogether. In my opinion, for what it is worth, we are still "waiting" for these people as they partake in our presence, which is consistent with the spirit of what Paul is advocating here. In the end, however, it remains a judgment call from the church leadership as to a second offering of the Lord's Supper; if they do allow this, this verse (11:33) does not condemn them for it.

115 "Gifts," when the word is used literally (as in 12:4) and is not implied, comes from the Greek charisma, meaning a spiritual endowment of some kind, or a "divine gratuity" or gift (Strong, *Dictionary* [electronic], G5486). From this we derive the word "charismatic," which refers to a person who believes that he practices the "gifts" of the Spirit. Incidentally, "spiritual gifts" is an appropriate phrase; "charismatic gifts" is redundant.

116 For further study on the Holy Spirit, I recommend my book, *The Holy Spirit of God: A Biblical Perspective* (Spiritbuilding Publishers, 2010); go to www.spiritbuilding.com/chad.

117 The phrase "to each one is given" does not require that every member of the Corinthian church receive some miraculous ability. God's Spirit chooses those to whom He wishes to impart His gifts; some will be excluded. There is no evidence, for example, that Titus, Luke, or several other of Paul's regular traveling companions had such ability; however, Barnabas (Acts 14:3) and Silas (Acts 15:32) did have gifts. Timothy may have had this ability (see 2 Tim. 1:6), but we see no demonstration of it; it is possible that his "gift" was for spiritual strength, not to work a visible miracle. Most telling is later in chapter 12, where Paul says, "All are not workers of gifts, are they?" (12:29).

118 In my opinion, for what it is worth, this was Timothy's "gift" (2 Tim. 1:6); see my *1 & 2 Timothy Commentary* (Spiritbuilding Publishers, 2024) for further explanation; go to www.spiritbuilding.com/chad.

119 Strong, *Dictionary* (electronic), G1100.

120 Robertson, *Word Pictures,* 170.

121 The fact that this collective baptism was represented by a handful of men—first, the apostles representing the Jews (Acts 2), then Cornelius and company representing the Gentiles (Acts 10)—does not change what has been done. The Spirit is not still performing a miraculous baptism of His own; what He did once for each group is sufficient for all time and for all people. The Spirit has already made acceptable both groups of people (Jews and Gentiles); people in both groups now can have salvation through the same gospel (2 Thess. 2:13–14). Upon entering into a covenant agreement with God through each person's baptism in water, both collective groups (Jews and Gentiles) become "one new man, thus establishing peace" (Eph. 2:15).

122 Barrett, *Epistles*, 289.

123 "The baptism is that commanded by Christ and the Holy Spirit, but inasmuch as it is done by the disciples under the direction of the Holy Spirit, it is said that the Spirit baptizes" (Lipscomb, *First Corinthians*, 185). Grosheide says: "Baptism receives significance only if there is an activity of the Spirit ..." (*Commentary*, 293), which makes sense if he means that one's water baptism must be accompanied by the Spirit's approval (Rom. 8:16).

124 Hodge, *Commentary* [electronic], on 12:31.

125 The phrase, "tongues ... of angels," has fueled the idea (especially among modern charismatics) that those who are endued with miraculous gifts can speak in a heavenly language that no one else can understand. And this has led to the idea that angelic tongues do not need to be understood, explained, or interpreted. All of this takes unwarranted liberty to all that Paul is saying in this passage. First, if angels do have their own language—and they probably do, since I doubt they speak in English or, say, Latin—that is their business. Second, Paul is not saying that we know what that angelic language is; he simply says if (hypothetically) someone was able to speak it without love, then it would still be a useless noise. Third, in every angelic encounter in the Bible in which angels have spoken, the ones hearing them always understood them in their own language, not in some angelic tongue. And finally, to intentionally try to mimic angelic tongue (in the form of ecstatic gibberish, which is what modern "speaking in tongues" sounds like) not only makes a mockery of God's gifts, but also makes a fool of the one fraudulently claiming to have them.

126 Barclay, *Letters*, 144.

127 To this point: it is significant to note that tongue–speaking—a subject on which Paul spends (proportionately) a great deal of time—is mentioned nowhere else in any of his epistles, or anywhere in the NT other than in Acts. Thus, tongue–speaking, as a representative of all spiritual gifts, was not meant to dominate our attention or the work of the church, but served the early church. "If the Pentecostal gift of tongues were for us today, none of our missionaries would have to spend any time in language study. They could then go to a foreign land and immediately begin preaching to the people in their own language without any previous preparation. The Apostles did just this on the day of Pentecost [Acts 2:4–11]" (DeHaan, *Studies*, 148).

128 "That image presented in this statement would be even more vivid for the Corinthians than it is for us. Corinth was famous for its manufacture of mirrors. But the modern mirror as we know it, with its perfect reflection, did not emerge until the thirteenth century. The Corinthian mirror was made of highly polished metal and, even at its best, gave but an imperfect reflection" (Barclay, *Letters*, 147).

129 JFB, *Commentary* (electronic), on 14:1; emphases are theirs.

130 Strong, *Dictionary* (electronic), G3874.

131 The citation, from Isa. 28:11, refers to the language of Israel's future captors, the Assyrians. To the Israelite captives, the Assyrian language was an unintelligible bunch of sounds.

132 The silence [Greek, *sigao*] here specifically refers to the act of tongue-speaking; it is the exact same Greek word used in reference to wives interrupting the church service to ask their husbands questions (14:34).

133 "The word [for "confusion" here] was used to describe political insurrections and revolutions; hence, it denotes a state of confusion, conflict, and disorder" (Willis, *Commentary*, 511; bracketed words are mine).

134 Some Bible versions, such as the ASV and ESV, move this last phrase to the following verse, so as to read: "As in all the church of the saints, the women are to keep silent in the churches …" (14:33b–34a). The Greek does allow for this grammatically, since the original Greek manuscripts have no punctuation. In my opinion, however, this view makes Paul inexplicably redundant, since he mentions again "in the churches" regarding women immediately after this. Furthermore, it does not really change anything regarding the discussion of women in the assembly.

135 Strong, *Dictionary* (electronic), G1135.

136 "Obviously, Paul is not restricting women from speaking when they worship God. Rather he is saying that they should respect their husbands in accordance with the Law" (Kistemaker, *1 Corinthians*, 512).

137 In other congregations, men were teaching that the resurrection of the saints had already occurred (2 Tim. 2:16–18), or that those who had already died would not participate in the resurrection at all—and thus will be lost (1 Thess. 4:13–14).

138 Though he does not pursue it here (because his emphasis is on the resurrection), Paul makes an important point: Christ did not just die, but He died for a particular reason, according to a specific prophecy, and as an act of His own volition. He died "for our sins," that is, as a perfect atonement offering that would remove forever the sins of those who believed in Him (Eph. 1:7, Col. 1:13–14, and Heb. 9:11–26). Not only this, but He really died, which defies bogus theories that Jesus was not dead when He was taken down from the cross (a.k.a. "swoon theory") (Coffman, *Commentary*, 250–251). No one buries a living body, but only a dead one; the fact that He was buried indicates that everyone involved in or having observed His crucifixion knew He was dead (Mark 15:42–46).

139 "[A]ccording to the Scriptures" refers not to the NT but the OT (as in, technically, 2 Tim. 3:16–17). This agrees with what Jesus said of Himself (Luke 24:26–27, 44–46). Paul also said this in his defense before Herod Agrippa II (Acts 26:22–23).

140 Barclay, *Letters*, 165–166; bracketed words are mine.

141 This list is from F. W. Farrar, "1 Corinthians," *The Pulpit Commentary*, vol. 19, H. D. M. Spence and Joseph Exell, eds. (Peabody, MA: Hendrickson Publishers, no date), 484; bracketed words are mine.

142 "Those Corinthians who denied the resurrection also failed to realize Christ's triumph over death, for He holds the keys of death and the grave (Rev. 1:18)" (Kistemaker, *1 Corinthians*, 554).

143 Lenski, *Interpretation*, 659.

144 "First fruits" [Greek, *aparche*] refers to the beginning of a sacrifice, or the first of something of a kind (see Rom. 8:23 and 1 Cor. 16:15) (Strong, *Dictionary* [electronic], G536). There are two thoughts here: First, the first fruits of the harvest means that there is more harvest coming; this principle has been used elsewhere regarding the Jews being the "first fruits" of all those who believe in Christ (James 1:18). Second, the blessing of a worthy representative of the group extends to what becomes the entire group (Rom. 11:16, Rev. 14:4); similarly, according to the Law of Moses, the offering of the first fruits of the harvest sanctified the entire harvest (Exod. 23:14–19, Lev. 2:12, 23:10, etc.). Christ being the "first fruits of those who are asleep [dead]" means that more will be raised as He was, and it is the Son of God who will raise them.

145 Even this explanation, however, seems unsatisfactory to some. Paul may have been referring to a custom among the Corinthians that he chose not to explain for the rest of us. Barclay thinks there was a belief among the Corinthians that they could be baptized vicariously for those who had died outside the Lord, much as Mormons believe today; if so, Paul does not give any approval to this practice, he only says that it is pointless if there is no resurrection of the dead (Barclay, *Letters*, 181).

146 Paul quotes from Hosea 13:14, where God summons "Death" and "Sheol" to unleash their "sting" against unfaithful Israel. Here, however, he turns this around and poses a rhetorical question—in essence, "What of your victory, O Death?—it is nothing against the power of Christ." See also Acts 2:24, 2 Tim 1:10, and Heb 2:14–15.

147 JFB, *Commentary* (electronic), on 15:56.

148 Kistemaker, *1 Corinthians*, 593–594. This follows the "Now concerning" formula Paul has been using throughout this epistle to respond to questions put to him in writing (e.g., 7:1). It is also important to note that this collection is "for the saints"—it is from the saints, and only for the saints. Nowhere in the NT do we see money collected by the saints being used for any purpose other than directly for saints who are in need. The modern denominational idea that churches are to collect money for those who are not Christians, social causes, or secular purposes is completely foreign to the NT pattern. Likewise, we never see Paul solicit money from non–believers, as we see today in the form of bake sales, rummage sales, firework stands, and other "fundraisers" for church work.

149 It is a mistake to call these contributions "tithes." A "tithe" [lit., tenth] is what God required in His covenant with Israel; we are no longer under that covenant, and this amount is no longer binding upon us. We do not give a "tithe"; we take up a collection or offering; each individual believer determines his own contribution. This amount can be more than, less than, or equal to 10%.

150 The Greek word here [*andrizesthe*] is used nowhere else in the NT and is derived from the root word [*aner*] for "man" or "men." Thus, while sometimes Paul says "men" in a general sense (irrespective of gender, as in 1 Tim. 2:2), here he means specifically male persons. Literally, the Greek word means "play the man; show yourselves men; act manly"—something

we must not expect a woman to do (Strong, *Dictionary*, G407 [electronic]; Robertson, *Word Pictures*, 202).

151 Strong, *Dictionary* (electronic), G331.

152 "Maranatha" is literally two words in Aramaic: *Maran* ("Our Lord") + *atha* ("come" or "has come"). Greek word definitions on this section are from Robertson, *Word Pictures*, 203–204, and W. E. Vine, *Expository Dictionary of New Testament Words*, vol. 3 (*STBC*, orig. 1952), 41–42.

www.ingramcontent.com/pod-product-compliance
Lightning Source LLC
LaVergne TN
LVHW010318070426
835508LV00033B/3493